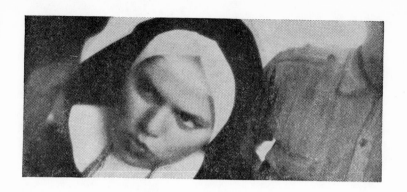

3 VOCATIONAL PERSPECTIVES SERIES

*

BY GABRIEL MARIE GARRONE

THE NUN:
SACRAMENT OF GOD'S SAVING PRESENCE

alba house
DIVISION OF THE SOCIETY OF ST. PAUL
STATEN ISLAND, N.Y. 10314

Translated by Paul D. Collins

This book was first published by Editions Fleurus, Paris, under the title *La Religieuse, Signe de Dieu dans le Monde*.

Nihil Obstat: John A. Goodwine, J.C.D.

Censor Librorum

Imprimatur: ✠ Terence J. Cooke, D.D., V.G.

New York, N.Y. February 9, 1967

The Nihil Obstat and Imprimatur are official declarations that a book or pamphlet is free of doctrinal or moral error. No implication is contained therein that those who have granted the nihil obstat and imprimatur agree with the contents, opinions or statements expressed.

Library of Congress Catalog Card No. 67-21423

Designed, printed and bound in the U.S.A. by the Pauline Fathers and Brothers at Staten Island, N.Y., as a part of their communications apostolate.

CONTENTS

INTRODUCTION

THE NECESSITY OF RECOLLECTION

Why these pages?

To aid your monthly retreats.

To give a continuity to the retreat addresses when such are included in the day's exercises.

To assure that no community, however remote, no religious, hindered by her duties, be deprived of this aid.

To hold out to all communities, all religious, the chance to feel closely united with one another and to be supported by a deep and intimate community of thought and prayer. Such reasons are clear and serious and each of you understands them.

So much is at stake!

Even when one is espoused and sincerely given to God, it is so easy to be pulled away from him by one's self or by the tyranny of work, and little by little to become incapable of meditation.

One's head is empty or too full.

One's work is urgent, overwhelming.

We lose the taste and feeling for silence and prayer.

What is a religious without prayer? What sort of soul can be vowed to God and let him become a stranger, inaccessible, to grow unable to talk with him or hear him or remain with him in silence, or to find the fundamental living contact with him that inspires action?

God is deprived of the best of what has been offered him: the profound attention of heart and soul. Alas, everything is possible, even the worst.

A religious incapable of recollection always suffers, for God lets her know the loss of his support, and her work lacks the very thing that makes it worthwhile: for despite appearances, the absence of prayer is a sure sign that love has grown cold. For his reign, God has such great need of the love of those whom he has chosen.

Therefore I wish that these conferences may be a useful, precious aid and admonition — indeed a rescue — to each community and to each religious.

May it be for you one more sign of God's care, a recalling of the promises and demands of your wonderful vocation, and a means of making you all aware of a unity, despite diversities of character, in the common goal of the kingdom of God.

There is *such* need that you be holy, faithful, united!

There are so many obstacles to the kingdom of God to be overcome in the places where he has called you to work, yet there are so many men of good will who look for your help and prayers and example. If only you are aware of your possibilities.

1

VOCATION

A NEW DAY FOR RELIGIOUS

What joy and confidence you must take in feeling yourselves more and more deeply *in* the Church

It seems to me that during these past ten years we have
progressed a century in respect to women's orders: for the
Holy Spirit has been blowing with such force outside the
communities, while inside he has been at work plowing up
and arousing them afresh to great new and necessary works
not until now undertaken.

There have been repeated and solemn words from the
sovereign pontiffs. To teachers and nurses there have been
countless addresses full of affection, counsel and light. New
measures have been initiated and further steps taken in the
direction of a deeper and wider program and a closer col-
laboration. There have been regular meetings of specialized
groups; Congresses; the publication of reviews; even "summit-
meetings". It seems to me that your availability and your
obedience have let you make great strides and that you are
now far ahead. Your strength lies in solidarity: solidarity
among yourselves and day by day a more complete solidarity
with the apostolic activity of the church, with Rome and
with your dioceses. Even as important auxiliaries, you have
been not merely on the fringe of it: you were and are at
its heart, at the center and source of its action.

During these past ten years you and all of us have known
the wonders that grace works when one accepts its leadings.

I shall not say more about it. You have experienced it, and even greater things remain in store for you.

From such a standpoint, how could there be any room for such uncertainty and anxious questions as, should we volunteer? how will we get others to join us? Such questionings are unworthy obstacles to grace. Keep the dignity and security of your religious state, for you know that the Church esteems it and you see what the Church does with it. Let me repeat: the Church needs you more than ever. Above all, she needs to see God in you. In a world in which God seems ineffective or nonexistent, she needs you as signs of him. More than anyone else, you must become (in fact you are) his symbols; but you will be so only if the reality is there behind the token. It is the hour of the religious in the life of the Church.

* * *

It is your hour because it is the hour for *poverty*. Poverty is what the world expects and cries out for, and it is perhaps the one aspect of your calling that men appreciate. Show them this poverty, the true poverty of those for whom God is enough, who count on him alone and never on money.

It is your hour because it is the hour for *obedience*. The world does not understand obedience: it refuses it and considers it a slavery. Show them that it is a love. "To obey is to love: it is the purest, loftiest, most disinterested, adoring, perfect act of love" (de Foucauld). Show this obedience, true, simple, bittersweet, by which the obedience of him who loved the Father even unto death becomes a reality in the heart of man.

Superiors and Sisters, this is how you must understand it. The outside world may not understand it right away, but anything less can only mislead as to what obedience is.

It is your hour because it is the hour for *chastity*. Despite hatred, cynicism, and the wild charges brought against it, do not be dismayed: for every decent and good-willed man is capable in his heart of appreciating it. Chastity is the human word for total attachment to Jesus Christ. Show them that one can be chaste, not by refusing to love, but *because* one loves. Let them be aware of your chastity, simple and complete, and let them know its reason.

Again, it is your hour because it is the Church's hour. By your community life and constitutions you are a portion of the visible Church. In revealing Jesus Christ, who is your life, you inevitably and immediately reveal the Church as well. How necessary this part of your mission is today! Others, even of perfect lives, cannot reveal it as directly as you; and this is your special honor. Be confident. Do not wonder how to survive. Seek to live, and then you will survive. Do not try first of all to win people to God, but rather so to dispose yourselves that *he* may call them. *"Seek first the kingdom of God . . . and all these things shall be given you besides."* That is a promise made by God.

BE WHAT YOU ARE

My dear Sister, you feel that the mission in which you have undertaken to work is doubly yours: yours because God's purposes are yours, and yours also because the best of your own gifts are going into your work to make it fruitful. Grace attaches you to God as it does to your unique reason for living. God is sufficient for you: it is that that has made you a religious. And it is that that God wants to say through you to a world that deems him useless and all the other things — money, pleasures, independence — indispensable.

Our mission must reach to the very heart of this world from which God is absent; it must make clear the missionary aspect of every real apostolate of today and face it boldly; but this will be possible only if we are able to make the name of God resound in the void. Who can do it better than you? You are not called to preach, my dear Sister, but to live and to let God be seen in you.

For your work during the coming months, what better intention could there be than this: Do all with the purpose of being what you are? Realize, deepen, and complete within yourselves the work of God who has chosen you and wants you for himself alone.

Remind yourself that for innumerable souls God does not exist. Remind yourself also that these souls say: "bread is necessary for life and it is not God who gives the bread"; "it is impossible to live without some enjoyment of life but it is not God who provides the pleasures"; "man is made to be his own master and God is but his unreasonable rival."

God does not provide bread! My dear Sister, because of those who thus blaspheme our Father, I ask you to be as you have promised: *poor.* I ask you to make an act of faith in this Father who gives his children their daily bread, and to offer him such interior and exterior acts of renunciation as his grace may inspire. Offer now a month of real poverty, of self-abandonment to providence, and of daring generosity such as to compensate for the world's dreadful lack of trust and to prepare the ground for the conversion of souls.

God does not provide pleasures! Because of all those whose spirits are growing corrupt and dissipated in pursuit of joyless pleasures, and who see in God an obstacle to happiness, be as you have promised: *chaste*. With Our Lady, offer your delicate, simple, joyous purity: let God alone fill your heart.

God is the unreasonable rival of man! Offer then a life in which you are wholeheartedly, knowingly, and joyfully submissive to the will of God in *obedience*. Here again, be as you have promised. Take care to be prompt and candid in every answer to the call of a God who liberates, rather than enslaves as does the world. How many ties there are to be broken and how many fine ways of service there are.

In speaking thus to you, my Sister, without knowing you, I realize that I am touching at the very heart of your life, but it is to ask you to yield it to God. I ask more than the intentions of your prayers and more than a temporary effort, but I know simply that I ask in God's name.

When you have accomplished your task and brought home to us your talents, I trust that you yourself may feel closer to God. When you have given to your mission not only your efforts but yourself, you will have become a little more what God made you for and wishes you to be.

THE HONOR OF GOD

A sad new feature peculiar to our times is cynical and public disrespect for God. The honor of God is no longer important. The word "blasphemy" is out of fashion and hardly in serious use. Each man may think and say what he pleases about God and indulge in sarcasm and insults. Of course, they say, individual consciences are to be respected, and the private beliefs of families and churches too; but the public forum, i.e., the press, the theatre, films, etc., belongs to everyone. Let God defend himself there if he finds any champions. Meanwhile all are free to attack him.

Thus it is by no means rare nowadays to see him become the target of defiance or of curses or mockery. Yesterday the Church bore the blows for him; today the attack is direct. The worst of it is not the terrible attacks on the honor of God but the fact that his own people have grown used to them. They discuss the talents of an author whose play they have just seen without remembering that the play was an insult to God. All sorts of excuses are made for this unfaithfulness of lax condonation: politics, politeness, art, freedom of expression, inability to speak out.

Will God put up forever with the indifference of his own people? Will they themselves long be able to keep a living religion in their hearts while they shockingly and scandalously fail to uphold his honor, and indeed act as accomplices of his enemies?

"*You dishonor me*" (John 8, 49). Our Lord's protest is unnerving and commanding as it rings in our ears, and one is inclined to continue by putting on his lips the words of Job, "Oh you my friends". Yes indeed, nowadays for all "friends of God", including the religious, there is a grave and urgent duty of reparation. We must make reparation for the hateful attacks on the honor of God around us and among us.

How to make reparation? A devout heart does not ask the question. The suffering itself, when an attack made on the honor of God wounds the Christian, is a reparation. It is the first and the best. However, one must take care: for alas, one gets used to anything. Still, in this duty of reparation there are all sorts of demands upon a soul who prays seriously, "hallowed be thy name." There are first of all the burden to be accepted and the foreseen indifference.

The mystery of the rejected love of this God whom men insult and affront in a tremendous defiance is for us no remote enigma: for before our eyes and in our hearts we have the image of a man scorned, spat upon, and insulted even on the cross where they nailed him — this Jesus whom we believe to be the Lord. It is at the foot of the cross that the loving soul makes reparation, for it is there that we see our God and the insults as well. It is there too that we discover in ourselves resources of reparation, there at the foot of the cross and also before the tabernacle, where the Body offered for us by our Lord is present, forever the gathering place of faithful souls to whom the honor of God is more than everything.

Beyond this there are many ways of reparation. To begin with, one must seek to fathom ever more deeply this honor of God to which the world and even Christians are becoming indifferent and heedless.

The Church is keenly perceptive of it and points the way: the liturgy, in words and in actions, in chants and in silences, shows how we are to understand "the glory of God" and how a soul can be nourished by this inexhaustibly delicate blend of love with what Holy Scripture calls "the fear of God." To recite the Psalms as the Church does is to renew at its very source one's sense of the honor of God.

However reparation is not only suffering or prayer. It means also, and perhaps primarily nowadays, the making of an act of faith, the affirmation that the more daringly God is denied by the world, the stronger he is in himself. If we are not careful the wound made in us by atheistic blasphemy can fester and infect our bloodstreams with germs of doubt, timidity or fear.

To make reparation is to make a strong act of faith in the God whom the world denies; it is not to bow the head but to lift it up; it is to make recompense by the courageous loyalty of a faith more vibrant than ever. Remember too that one believes not merely with the lips or even the heart: one believes, as one denies, by one's way of life (cfr. Titus 1, 16). In this respect the religious has a considerable mission in the world of today: to honor God and to honor him in the face of the world. Who can do it better than she?

Let all souls consecrated to our Lord renew their sense of vocation and grasp once more the fundamental meanings of their vows. Let them see their chance, by real poverty, chastity and obedience, to show the world that God exists because they live by him, and to tell the world what God is, the source of both happiness and love.

Our Father, who art in heaven, may thy name be hallowed by the souls whom thou hast chosen for thyself alone. Let them see the breadth of opportunities in their mission. Give them a taste of thine infinite sweetness.

2

THE INTERIOR SELF

FAITH

Faith is the foundation and root of the whole spiritual life. These two familiar figures are used forcefully and repeatedly by St. Paul: *"Have Christ dwelling through faith in your hearts ... rooted and grounded in love"* (Eph. 4, 17). That means that if faith is vigorous, all is alive; if it grows anemic, nothing thrives. For it is by faith that we are related to the infinite God. Faith provides the object of our love and *"is the substance of things to be hoped for"* (Hebr. 11, 1). Whom do we love? he whom faith makes known to us. What do we hope for? that which faith lets us see. Faith alone.

By no purely human means can we attain to knowledge of the mystery of God, and the inner life and relations of the divine persons of the Trinity are closed to us. "No one has at any time seen God." *"No one can come to me unless the Father who sent me draw him"* (John 1, 18; 6, 44). Here below, it is by the gift of faith that the Father draws us, and faith establishes the contact between our souls and Christ in whom the divine mystery clearly shines forth. By faith alone.

That is why faith is as precious and delicate a treasure as is life itself (cf. II Cor. 4, 7). That is why God deals with our faith according to laws that we do not grasp and which constantly make difficult demands on our assent. To live by faith is to consent to live by God's promises. It is to accept everything: this present life so disconcerting and disappointing, and eternal life so far off and incredible. It is to agree and admit that God is right, however things may seem, and that what he pronounces and promises is Truth. To live by faith means that, no more, no less; it is costly and difficult but it is imperative.

We cannot enter into the mystery of God without his will and favor, so we must strive — against our inclinations — to rely entirely upon a vision which is not our own. This naturally goes against our natures.

Furthermore, the more faithful we grow, the more God's grace tries our faith to perfect it. Consider the saints, especially Thérèse of Lisieux. The more we try to live by faith, the more God takes us at our word and makes us depend solely on himself. We often take that as too severe a test and are tempted to complain. But if we are truly living by faith, God will call us to do so more and more completely. "I believe what I want to," said St. Thérèse to disconcert those who supposed her to be simply ecstatic and to encourage those who might follow her in "the narrow way" which was open to all.

Strange as it may seem, that is everyone's path. We forget that we do not walk alone and that God is with us. The faith which demands so much strength, which we must work so hard to develop, is the gift of God. *"We all . . . are being transformed into his very image from glory to glory as by the Spirit of the Lord"* (II Cor. 3, 18). It is not only something planted in us to be guarded and cultivated, to be cherished even if it makes us suffer; it is a divine tie, like a leash that God has attached to us to draw us after him.

Many difficulties in our faith and the good and salutary tests to which it is put are increased and made unduly complicated — or even catastrophic — by our own fault; because we forget that faith is above all the gift of God. If the virtues are divine gifts, so by far is faith.

So it is on God that we must count when (by his providence) human supports prove weak, human guarantees of the faith seem to be lacking, and even the desire to go on believing grows cold. It is then that we must ask God to hold us fast by his hand. We are walking on water and upheld by the voice of our Lord. If "common sense" tells us that we are not on dry land, let us stand up straighter, lest we sink, for God is holding us. Pray when faith draws us away and the light of this world goes out.

This does not mean that work is unnecessary.

The faith which waits for the light and enables us to bear the delaying of a clear vision does not dispense us from the exercise of every effort within us.

First of all we owe it to the honor of God to make sure that the light of faith and reason are always in accord, for Reason is his too. Besides, it is necessary for us. We must not consider faith as a strange superhuman phenomenon; the facts of life must be harmonized with the truths of faith and the apparent contradictions resolved in our minds if we are to keep our sanity; the diverse truths of the faith must little by little be arranged in a pattern that is ever more coherent and ordered. This has been the Church's way over the centuries and we do well to follow it.

After all, you must *be ready always with an answer to everyone who asks a reason for the hope that is in you*" (I Pet. 3, 15), for you are Christ's messenger to him especially if you are engaged in any sort of teaching work. This is why the Church today wishes all nuns to study and learn to cultivate their intellectual grasp of the faith with no less serious perseverance than they give to purely spiritual exercises.

May your faith be a living one, for *"he who is just lives by faith"* (Rom. 1, 17).

NOTHING IS IMPOSSIBLE WITH GOD

These are familiar words of Holy Scripture and Mary heard them in the message of the angel revealing her extraordinary destiny. Do we realize that these words are meant for us too as we face a destiny whose human dimensions may perhaps be estimated but whose supernatural reality infinitely surpasses our powers? We all need to hear again those words, for they can save us from despair or from reducing our spiritual ambitions to the mediocre level of what is merely humanly possible. Alas, it is so common to hear it said, "God does not demand the impossible." But yes, God *does* demand the impossible.

It is enough to know it as a fact and not to count on our own powers in learning the difficult art of relying on God alone. And if God asks the impossible, it is that he intends to accomplish it.

The Christian vocation, and at its core the religious vocation, are completely lost when they seem to be easy, accessible, or reasonable in the trite human sense of the words — or even in a lofty sense. If we are able to climb to the level of the Christian and religious life by our own powers, if we can pull ourselves up by the strength of our arms, then we have mistaken the goal. To reach God, to learn his secrets, to delight in his presence, and to know the love of the heart of Jesus, we must be lifted up by him (cf. Matt. 11, 27; Phil. 2, 5).

We need a Savior. To forget it is to lose all, and alas, we are forgetful. Because we so often fall short and our weakness dismays and hinders us, little by little we tend to create a vague dream of a state of peace, stability, and assurance which would lift us above ourselves.

However, what is good and true and sure is to feel the need of Christ, as did St. Paul, crying passionately out of weakness for which Christ was the only answer: *"Unhappy man that I am! Who will deliver me from the body of this death?"* (Rom. 7, 24)

The Christian's real assurance lies in his experiencing, accepting, and maintaining a sense of need of a Savior. Only in this way can we formulate a right idea of the greatness and reality of our vocation; then only can we seriously and literally call ourselves children of God, *"and such we are"* (Eph. 2, 4; 3, 20; I John 3, 1). What God asks is impossible because it is truly nothing else than to be like him and united with him

Thus poverty amounts to wealth.

We can become sons of God only by his making us so. Consequently the best of our interior efforts ought to be spent in cultivating this dependence on God and our Savior Jesus Christ and his grace. We may do so by humility, by prayer — of petition as well as adoration, and by obedience.

From this viewpoint our protests and resistances to the demands of the religious life when they thwart or humble us seem very petty and unbecoming. In fact they are absurd if they do not cause us to need Jesus more. For when he does become more necessary to us, then no other good is comparable. Thank God if he carves out his place in our hearts and solders a line between our helplessness and his omnipotence.

The appreciation of our impotence is the real deliverance, and then everything becomes possible — not to us but to God in us. Then the real wisdom of the old saying, "God does not ask the impossible," becomes clear. I can do no more, therefore God is not asking more. The ordering of grace has changed the sense of the adage, for the law of that realm is: God wills it, therefore it is possible. We see the possibility only when we have closed our eyes to appearances and begun to give credit to God alone. The possibility is not really our own but God's. If we keep looking at our feet, we will not take a step; but if we deliberately look across the precipice to where God waits and holds out his hand, we will soon find ourselves on the other side, thanks to him.

The effort of faith is the primary, most necessary, and often the costliest one, but it makes everything else effective. That is where to begin.

What does God will? How is his will known? That is the real question. When we know its answer, the rest will follow. It is possible if he wills it. The saints have always sought it and this accounts for their prudence, reflectiveness, and the absence of haste as well as for their marvellous boldness and limitless ambitions and eventual rewards. But we must know what God wills and not simply throw ourselves upon his providence.

What *does* God will? that we be saints, that each one of us be holy. He wishes it, so it is possible. Do you understand? Will you take this seriously for a change?

What does he want? There is so much left to be done in the Church, so many opportunities for service, so many unhappy people that need to be cared for. God wishes you to be anxious over those who find nowhere to turn in their troubles, for this is an essential part of our pastoral ministry.

Certainly God wills it and it is certainly possible. When I look at some bitterly crying need, I often think of the generous strength stored up in so many devout hearts in so many communities and wonder why you hesitate. God wills it. You cannot do it? then try and see whether he can do it. Our Lord still works miracles: who knows what he might do through you? Nothing is impossible with God.

The God who conquers death in his resurrection, who sits at the right hand of the Father and intercedes for us, who comes to us with his Holy Spirit in tongues of fire, who makes himself bread to be eaten, whose heart was pierced by a spear to let the last drops of blood flow out before our eyes — let him convince you. What more do we need to assure us that we are loved and to dare us to serve such a love?

HOPE

The evils of our society and the dangers to faith and charity are perhaps most clearly exposed under the bright light of hope.

This thought struck me during a recent retreat for a group of nuns. Joined with them in silence and prayer in the presence of God, I seemed to see better the risks run today by hope, which is so essential to holiness. I saw better also, with keen admiration, the marvellous ground that the religious life with its vows offers for this virtue, and indirectly, the great door it opens to clearer experience of the Father's love.

How quickly nowadays people get discouraged and lose

confidence. How little it takes to turn lively enthusiasm into dull depression: it happens easily when we are upset or disappointed or tired out, or it can be caused by boredom with the chores of daily routine.

We must guard and cherish hope and not resign ourselves to its wanings; for it is a virtue that takes second place to none, and God absolutely needs it in his plans for us. Cherish it, for it is indispensable.

Do not take superficial failures to heart: a scaffold may fall while the house remains standing. Indeed scaffolding is naturally dropped as the work is completed and can stand alone.

When the body grows weak and we lose the self-confidence that animates our lives, when we cannot participate in community affairs and miss the support that comes from familiar companionship and common tasks, we feel at a loss, out of things, and get emotionally upset. But such disturbing emotions (which God does not spare us, for we must learn to get over them) cannot really upset us unless a serious malady has already taken root.

When prayer weakens or stops, the real danger begins and hope is very much at stake. Hope is animated when one prays and, far from being dashed by trivial reverses, is increased instead of diminished. We must be watchful: if our prayers dwindle, our hope is in a bad way. If we don't take care, faith and charity will suffer too, for they are joined to hope.

What shall we do about it? Of course we shall examine ourselves to see what the source of the trouble may be; but above all we must seek to deepen and increase the faith that nourishes hope and the charity which is its flowering.

Hope is traditionally likened to a flower. Its roots must

be tended if a flower is to be fresh and beautiful. When hope becomes difficult, we must fall back on meditation: for divine mysteries renew hope. Its failures are always linked with deficiencies at prayer. To believe is to hope, and the more we live our religion the stronger our hope. Besides, the flower exists to produce fruit. Love is the fruit of hope, and when it is not produced naturally hope weakens. The flower barely survives when the heart is impure, when Jesus is not loved enough, or when his friends are not ours. To love is to hope.

Again, what more fertile ground for hope is there than the soul avowing poverty, chastity, and obedience?

Vowed to true poverty, an agreement to rely on God alone, not on money, and to jettison everything that suggests that he is not enough. . . .

Vowed to real chastity with willing heart and life, to be fulfilled only by Jesus. Human affections are precious and good: can we live without them? Yes, if Jesus is enough.

Given to true obedience, not of the sort that argues or makes reservations, but that surrenders the will to Jesus so completely that there is nothing left in one's own hands.

But what is all of that if hope does not thrive? Our Lord calls and beckons: we walk toward him with the trust of a love for the Lord who calls. We have discarded the world's keys to happiness, money, family life, personal independence, and are walking on water. What prospects! What a difference between the one who says with her lips and even her heart, "Our Father," and the other who says it by her life. Your vows are a complete and living *Our Father*. What glory for God! There's no truer, simpler or more direct experience of God on this earth. What a lesson too for a world that needs it so badly and will not learn in any other way. What a favor

God has granted you in giving you this calling to work in his vineyard, among his children.

THE WILL OF GOD

How simple the phrase is. It sounds best from the lips of the Blessed Virgin speaking without doubt or hesitation. On our own lips it has all sorts of nuances, depending on our own wills and moods, varying from hour to hour, arousing very different reactions. Still, it is the loveliest phrase that can be spoken: for it empties our hearts, so to speak, cleanses them of impurity, and reveals their real riches. It is also a hard phrase, which does not resound in our hearts and often provokes a rebellion. We shelter ourselves from its demands by raising a barrage of questions; we try to avoid it or run away from it under a smokescreen of obscure reasonings.

We must undertake to pray these words with the purest and warmest intentions, for they are the touchstone of our love for God. If they distress us, it must be that God distresses us. No matter what the exact object of the divine will is or the opposition that it may inspire in us, neither our opposition nor aversion can in the least affect it. It is never gentler or more loving than when it asks of Him what is hardest of all to give: *"My soul is sad, even unto death. . . . Let this cup pass away from me; yet not as I will, but as thou willest"* (Matt. 26, 38). "Behold I come . . . to do your will, O my God" (Ps. 39, 8). Never has God been loved more; never has his will so overwhelmed anyone; and he bore the burden of the sins of the whole world.

One could discuss indefinitely the apparent contradiction

of the soul who loves the will of God and finds unspeakable joy in performing it yet at the same time does so at brutal cost. But it is not something to be discussed: it is to be lived, and love is the secret of the contradiction. Difficult as it may be to imagine it, it exists nonetheless. We must so give ourselves to loving the will of God that it is ever in our thoughts and governs us.

Ever in our thoughts: these simple words will fulfill our lives if we keep them constantly in mind and heart. Hear them on our Lord's lips, repeat them with him as he speaks in his agony, recite them again and again in Psalm 118, as he did; look up the many passages in the Gospels, particularly St. John's, where Christ contemplates, accepts, and loves the will of him that sent him (cf. John 4, 34). It is amazing that hearts like ours are able to share in such a love; but by the grace of God, it is so.

Hear the words on our Lady's lips: she calls the divine will his "word" as the momentous invitation is announced to her. *"Be it done to me according to thy word"* (Luke 1, 38). And again, *"Mary kept in mind all these things, pondering them in her heart"* (Luke 2, 19).

That is the way we are enabled to put aside our own natural resistances to the divine will. The power of love is an intense flame that consumes the faulty and rebellious elements of our nature and wills.

The order of a superior: it is God's will. A certain task: it is God's will. An interior suffering to bear: it is God's will. A time will arrive when the pain of a sacrifice endured to the bitter end is mysteriously reconciled with the joy of loving the Father, in Christ, with Mary (cf. II Cor. 1, 8). We well know this is true despite all arguments to the contrary; and we know that we are not being honest when we

2 *The Nun:*

call it impossible and, by not trying, forfeit grace for ourselves and others.

"Our Father ... thy will be done." May you all know fully, in the reality of your service, the delights of those words our Lord taught us.

THE LOVE OF OUR LORD

Thanks to Charles de Foucauld, everyone nowadays knows the name of the abbé Huvelin, the holy Parisian priest who was responsible for his return to God and was his spiritual director.

The Love of our Lord is the title of a series of addresses by Huvelin, recorded by one of his listeners, and that same theme occurs repeatedly in the frequent correspondence between the hermit in the Sahara and his director in Paris. There was a wonderful accord between these two men who were so different yet so alike, so separated yet so close, the one lost in the crowd, the other alone in the desert; but the basis of this accord is brilliantly clear — the love of our Lord. How simple and great and powerful it is! The clear light of the devotion of these two men shines out from the pages and makes us wish that for us too everything could be reduced to their simple reality, the love of our Lord Jesus Christ.

What else do we need? Why are we always looking for new ideas and approaches, new stimuli? What a waste of time and effort. We must blow out the gutted candles that give more smoke than light and becloud our vision if we are going to imitate the desert father and his priest and eliminate everything but that tiny bright flame in us, like one before the tabernacle, the love of our Lord Jesus Christ.

* * *

Christ our Lord is given for us — delivered up. Holy
scripture uses the word often: the Father has delivered him
up for us ... he gives himself for us ... he lets himself be
delivered up for us. He gives his body and blood in double
sacrifice. As St. Paul said, *"How can he fail to grant us also
all things with him?"* (Rom. 8, 32).

Of course it is faith that convinces us of all that. But
it may also produce the false images and notions that keep
coming between us and Christ to make us forget him or
lead us to think that something more is needed, or indeed
to live as if his love were not enough for us.

What more can we want? What holds us back from
making full use of this utterly complete gift? What holds
us back is our inattention together with our shortcomings
and lack of courage.

In no respect does Christ limit the gift of himself; nowhere
does he refuse anyone access to all the riches he has in
store. He gives of himself as much as we are willing to receive, neither more nor less, for he offers all once and for
all. He himself says that if he has not done more, it is that
it is impossible to do more.

The Church knows it well and draws insatiably on this
inexhaustible treasury. She returns to the source again and
again and wishes all of us to see and know the Savior who
so desires to have his brethren share with him; and the
Church is never more avid than in Holy Week when our
Lord invites his friends to do so. The fulness of God's love
pours out of a heart torn with anguish upon his "little
children" gathered around him; it offers in sacrifice a love
that endures through agony until the end as the heart of

his flesh is pierced by a spear which lets fall the last drops of blood.

The Church accompanies him step by step from the Last Supper to the mount of Olives, from the garden to the praetorium — and to Calvary and the tomb. We find him again in the lovely light of Easter morning, sit with him before a fire where he cooks a fish and has some bread for us, or gather in the upper room where he seizes the hand of an apostle to thrust it into his wounded side.

All these are external events, but they indicate what the internal and intimate life of one vowed to God can be, one who undertakes not so much to love as to believe in his love and let herself be loved.

The religious is one who wishes God to be enough for her. It is in Christ that she finds the Father she seeks and to whom she gives herself. To love God and Jesus Christ is all one.

To love Christ is to learn the one path that leads to the Father, to know where and how to find it, to see it stretching to infinity — a path where every possibility is offered, everything is ours.

May his grace lead you to rediscover the simple meaning of the words, the love of Jesus Christ, and to be content with it in the proper sense of the word "content" — that you rejoice and wish for nothing else.

This is your right and your duty.

THE DESIRE FOR GOD

Our attachment to God is primarily the attachment of our will: to love God is to do what he asks and to live after his commandments (cf. I John). Without that it is pointless to talk of attachment to God, for it is a delusion or deception.

This is why we must guard against letting our love for God be governed by our feelings, as if it were a mere sentimental affair of the heart. The realm of feeling is above all the realm of instability and confusion.

If we love God simply with all our *heart*, there come a day when the heart lets us down: it is cold and we imagine that we no longer love him. This can lead both to discouragement and to hopelessly artifical efforts to revive and stimulate our poor affections.

And that is not the worst danger.

Loving God only with the heart, one may wake up one day and be astonished to find that the heart has transferred its affections to one of God's creatures — oneself or someone else — and it is often too late before we are aware of it. Alas, these transfers are very common: for the heart but feels, it does not see and cannot ward off illusions. To love God is to live after his commandments. That is how Jesus loved his Father (II John 6). That is the unmistakable sign. Only by such faithful obedience to the will of God can one tell whether love is real and firmly rooted in its proper ground, the will.

Must then sentiment be driven away, the heart silenced and not allowed to share in our love? No, for that would be madness; besides, it would be impossible. And it would work contrary to the will of God, who asks of us no such harsh asceticism or absurd deprivation.

The word *heart* as it is commonly used is easily misunderstand and often vulgarized or cheapened. But remember that it is frequently used in classical literature as well as in Holy Scripture in a lofty and noble sense fit to express love for God. There the heart is not mere sentiment.

When we speak of "a man of heart," we are not thinking of his warm feelings but of a certain nobility of spirit, an ability to put sentiment aside in favor of what is right and good, and when necessary, to give his complete devotion to a cause that is important.

When Holy Scripture in the vivid imagery of the Hebrew language centers a man's fundamental judgments and actions in his heart, it is obviously not referring to quick emotions but to the will, primarily if not exclusively. And our Lord speaks in the same sense in Matt. 15, 19 ff., *"For out of the heart come evil thoughts. . . ."*

Meanwhile the Church ascribes to the heart of our Lord the ineffable love toward the Father and us, from which stems our redemption.

It is up to us to coordinate the several sides of ourselves and come to love God as complete human beings, first with our wills then with our feelings. For the will which is not mere sentiment but the true home of a love which performs the will of God, does not exclude the heart but rather demands its aid.

It sometimes happens that the heart must be humbled or kept quiet. It also must be fed and led. It must love God: therefore it must look for God's good pleasure in everything, however one may feel about it. Furthermore, for the will's sake, the heart must try to find a real *taste for God*. St. Ignatius in particular demands this of all who would be reconverted; and the inspired prayer of Psalm 118 is that of a heart in sweet accord with the divine law.

A taste for God is obtained by prayer and effort and brings the soul many of its purest joys. It is acquired at

the price of renouncing many other tastes, good as they
may be, and sacrificing any incompatible ones. God must
capture our hearts. This figure of speech means one thing
in the world; but raised to a higher level, it can be just as
meaningful to those who are God's own. It implies the gentle
advances of a lover, the inviting charm, the needs created,
and the things in him to adore. Where love is true, it can
and must aspire to this desire for God. One must be cautious,
not to let it have the uppermost hand, but one can be
supported by it and use it with delight. Yet one must also
know how to do without it, if God pleases to show that it
is unessential.

"No one is happier than a real Christian," said Pascal
and thus by grace he rose above the misdirected errors of
Jansenism.

We must love God quite simply, being careful of our
hearts yet letting them speak. They will help up to respond
to God's desires and to please him.

I BELIEVE IN THE HOLY SPIRIT

The Church is revealed to the world on the morning of
Pentecost. The Spirit revives and excites the apostles and
his fire alights on them; *"we cannot but speak of what we
have seen and heard"* (Acts 4, 20). The same Spirit dwells
in the Church and is capable of the same things in forms
suitable to our times.

A mission is one of those works of the Spirit. We must
clearly appreciate that it is not a merely human effort to
arouse enthusiasm but it is the impact of grace. To believe
in the Holy Spirit means letting his power seize us; for there

are so many souls to be converted. *"J have come to cast fire upon the earth, and what will J but that it be kindled?"* (Luke 12, 49).

One never reads without some fresh astonishment the passages in Holy Scripture where our Lord announces the coming of the Holy Spirit: for we must admit that we have not yet taken this gift of God fully to heart, and are inclined to take it more as a figure of speech than a reality. The infinite measure of the gift tends to be reduced to what our reasons can conceive and interpret; and we act as if Christ at his Ascension had left us merely a promise.

Yet the Spirit was *given*, so fully and violently that the upper room was shaken, so penetratingly that the men there who spoke of Christ were no longer recognizable as those who had forsaken him and fled, and so definitely that the Church never lacks his power. And by the same signs of love of God and man, of boldness and humility, his very presence will be manifested until the end of time. Until the end of time, prayer that is unhesitant and persevering will retain its irresistable power. Until the end of time, the Spirit of God will shake the world with his impact and his creations, renewals and conversions.

Each of us carries the divine "germ," and God faces each of us with circumstances where its power is called into action. The power is like the fire that was seen when it took possession of the apostles: a rich and glowing inner fire, yet revealing its power to our eyes. It is a fire that consumes without appearing to do so and enkindles without our realizing its source. Or again, we see a sparkling flame and are drawn to it.

It is not a matter of choice, for the Spirit uses us as he

pleases. An indirect fire that warms without proclaiming its origin is nonetheless beneficial; and it is perhaps best for us when our apostolate takes such an indirect form, for otherwise souls are apt to grow attached to ourselves rather than to God.

The necessary thing is to believe in this presence of the Holy Spirit in us: for then our faith allows him to act. He is virtually unable to act until we have accepted the reality of his presence and action, or if we have not surrendered ourselves by faith to his use. We bear the Holy Spirit in us and it is he who must *act* in us and gradually mortify our carnal selves. He will lift up our hearts to the prayer which is Christ's, make us wonderfully radiant in charity, and substitute for the miserable *me* Christ himself who is my life.

We pray: but it is the Spirit who prays in us and who works at our very roots to make us like Christ.

We work: it is the Spirit who works through us to renew the face of the earth to the glory of God.

We suffer: it is the Spirit purifying and refining our mortal selves to prepare us for a new divine life.

Thus, to believe in the Holy Spirit is nothing but to know the reality of the heavenly gift.

It is a reality, not merely a promise. We call ourselves sons of God and so we are. May all that result not in sentimental or superficial aspirations but in a deep and complete turning to him. Such a renewal at its very source benefits not only the individual soul but the whole world, for it provides another and new stepping-stone to God. The Christian who believes that the Spirit of God dwells in him is a treasure for the world of men.

A nun who believes that what she has given to God has

been really taken by his Holy Spirit cannot fail to do wonders. Rather, God will do them through her. She does not necessarily have to be aware of their happening.

THE DEFENDER

Defender is the word preferred by many fine scholars in translating the texts of the Gospel where our Lord outlines the rôle of the Holy Spirit. The liturgy simply transcribes the original word as *Paraclete*.

He is someone near us, at our side, to support and sustain us; one who is there in our behalf much as a lawyer stands in court in behalf of his client. Thus the word *Advocate* is also traditionally used for the Holy Spirit.

In his manner of presenting to us the mission of the Holy Spirit, our Lord displays such a mercifully loving heart and gentle solicitude that we miss much if we fail to appreciate his tenderness so fully budding with hope.

When we speak of the tenderness and sweetness of the Spirit we are not to imagine anything coyly feminine: for this defender supports us in a combat. He aids the fighters, not the stragglers, and among his other names are "fire" and "flame." It is of course this external sign that chose for his first manifestation amid a rushing mighty wind. This defender is not consoler in the weak sense of that word, but one who helps us to conquer; he is not a solace for helplessness but a stimulant of energy.

In that light, nothing is more touching than the Master's lingering gaze at his own friends gathered around the table for the last time before his "hour," the hour of agony and separation.

Soon they will be alone and afraid and feel themselves orphaned. He anticipates it all as he looks at them — first, Peter the most ardent who will fall the farthest in his weakness, and then the others who will forsake him in the night.

Never did Jesus speak to them in more tender words, never had he shown in voice or conversation such profound emotion and affectionate care for these men, his own.

Will they remember what he told them?

Will they remember it when they are accused?

Will their faith be strong enough when they are called before a tribunal?

Will they believe that he is still with them even when they no longer see him? Will they understand that he is even more fully with them than before?

He knows that the answer must be, No. At least until the Holy Spirit comes to lift up their hearts and give them the strength of God himself.

That is why the Spirit of the Father, in Christ's thoughts and promises, is the bountiful answer to his friends' frailty and impotence.

Someone will always be there. Someone will repeat to them what their master could not make them grasp. Someone will whisper to them the words to say before the judges. Someone will fill them with a courage they never dreamed of. They will not be alone, orphaned. Someone will enable them to live as he lived and to know his affection for them and to say with all their hearts, "Father," to the Father of the unique Son.

This someone is the Holy Spirit.

Happy is the soul who listens to Jesus' words at the last supper and knows that they are meant for herself: for that evening he was thinking not only of the apostles but of all who through them would believe in him.

Indeed, what was true of the apostles is true of each of us. We all know what it is to forget our Lord's promises, to be frightened before an enemy, to be weak, and to feel lonely. But each of us shares in our Lord's most loving promise and in all the strength that it provides.

Come, Holy Spirit. . . .

Come, divine Defender. . . .

Come, sweet guest of the soul. . . .

Teach us to say, Father. Lead us to be as sensitive as St. Ignatius, the martyr, to the sound of the well-spring in the very center of our beings which keeps repeating the holy name.

OUR LADY

One must believe simply and firmly that Mary is truly the Mother of God; yet who can claim to have always faced up to the implications of this affirmation?

It conveys better than anything else the truths of the Incarnation, and the Council of Ephesus so devised it. It tells us with rather crude force what is to be believed: that that very Jesus, born of Mary, is truly the eternal Son of the Father.

What we can and must do is make an act of faith — faith in the reality of the Incarnation, in the reality that the Son of God was born of Mary and faithful unto death to her who bore him.

Directly because of this, Mary exists to help us to a deeper belief in our Savior. She obliges us to rise above the superficiality of a prayer addressed only to herself, when she is but a creature.

When we name her, "Holy Mary, Mother of God," we vigorously proclaim the very foundations of our faith, and accept all its blunt challenges, including that of the Jews who replied to our Lord's explanation of the holy Eucharist, *"This is a hard saying. Who can listen to it?"* (John 6, 61). Addressing Mary as Mother of God, we face our belief directly: God, born of a woman, has become one of us. His name is Jesus, whom *"we have heard, seen with our eyes, looked upon and our hands have handled"* (I John 1, 1).

The Blessed Virgin calls us to make an act of faith and to consider its implications. That is why it is so good to turn to her and why one is so well off with her. The graciousness that we find there is not simply the presence of human purity and goodness: it is the divine love itself. Faith gives it to us if we are willing to believe.

Mary believed first, and blessed is she among women. It is this blessedness that she invites us to know.

If our acts of faith are rightly made and dependent on her to reach our Lord, they will certainly send us back to her in gratitude for what she does for us. And all that we have been led to do for her will unfailingly lead us nearer her Son. She is completely maternal in his service. Her love for us with its attentive prayers and reminders leads us more deeply into her Son's Kingdom of love, where she was the first to enter.

Understood in its true meaning and purpose, our devotion to the Blessed Virgin cannot but develop into something infinitely delicate, simple, and humble.

The Church points the way. Here as in everything she

sets the pace and tone and enables us to discover that love for the Blessed Virgin can be wonderfully rich in devotion, admiration, generosity, and joy.

Led by the Virgin Mother the procession of the hand-maidens of the Lord goes forth to meet the bridegroom. *"He who finds me finds life"* (Prov. 8, 35). The Church uses these words of Wisdom in respect to our Lady.

The religious loves her by instinct and has never ceased plumbing the riches she represents. And how much more there is to discover.

THE MYSTERY OF LOURDES

Crowds have flocked to Lourdes from all over the world for many years now and they will continue. The grotto has seen some marvellous sights, but the most wonderful ones will be seen only in Heaven. Some unforgettable ones remain in our minds as full of glorious promise. There was the military pilgrimage when soldiers in their varied uniforms of yester-day's battles, of nations which had been enemies, found such a mutual friendship reborn in them under the gaze of our Lady that they spontaneously expressed it in open gestures of brotherhood. There was the pilgrimage of forlorn prostitutes whose spirits were manifestly remade through prayer to Mary, their broken bodies and sick souls mirac-ulously restored and animated with the freshness of youth. The great labor unions' pilgrimage came to be refreshed at Mary's springs, renewing a love that must be strong and a strength that must not cease to be loving.

All that was the smallest visible part of what is invisible. One never goes among those who are praying at the grotto, whether sick or well, without seeing a religious habit. The nuns are there, in twos or threes, in the various habits which show the diversities of the world and at the same time the unity of their vocations. They are there because the welfare of sinful man is important to them and because it is dearly important to the Church that nuns be there to pray for sinners.

Day after day Lourdes and its grotto are the scene of silent colloquies which beyond a doubt are rich and full of hope for all, especially the hope that links the Blessed Virgin and the kneeling women who remind one of Bernadette.

It seems to me impossible that a single nun could have knelt there praying silently or even simply sitting before the white statue of Mary in the rocks without it striking her as clear and evident and even thrilling that she is on the right track and that God has not misled her.

Every illusion fades away in this unique spot in the world. Illusions are not for those who are detached and self-sacrificing for the love of their Lord and their brethren. Illusion is not for those who agree to put all into the hands of God: heart, fortune, will. The real illusions threaten men and women who, having the use of some of God's goods, tend to let the goods suffice and to dispense with God.

It is always difficult to walk by faith and to take the risk of answering the voice which says, "Come," and walk unsupported on the water like St. Peter. It is a long journey in which troubles can arise and, through the emotions, gain our minds. Before Mary anxieties pass and all becomes luminous.

Blessed are the poor in spirit. Blessed are they who have left everything to follow Christ. Blessed are they who have seen Christ himself in the forlorn people who need them.

My dear sister, humbly on your knees before Mary, you see the evidence and cannot doubt that you are right: while asking everything of you, God has given you the better part. Make the most of this moment of light. Never forget it, and ready yourself for tomorrow.

And pray for your sisters, that they be faithful — or if necessary, that they become faithful once again. Pray that those who already bear in their hearts, whether they realize it or not, the marks of a divine call, may never refuse it.

It is impossible for so much good will to go without a response. The Blessed Virgin will have silently touched many souls, and tomorrow, when some young woman asks herself when she first received the grace that led her to be a nun, she will answer, "It was at Lourdes."

May St. Bernadette, loved by Mary, bring to all her sisters around the world the incomparable certainty that they too are loved, and a great eagerness to be worthy of it.

THE LOVE OF TRUTH

One of the greatest words of human language is Truth. And we know that it is one of the names of God: *"I am the truth,"* says our Lord. Failure in truth is one of the surest offenses to God, or even to cast doubts upon his word. But to accept as true every divine word and to keep truth all-important in our relations with God and our fellows and in self-examination is to offer him supreme homage.

We must often examine ourselves about this fundamental aspect of the Christian and religious life, for the "eye" of the soul is easily disconcerted or dulled (cf. St. Luke 11, 34).

Things become falsified, and into the bargain, we live in a world which conspires to make simplicity of outlook and expression difficult and rare.

Nevertheless we must be simple and direct if we wish to live in union with God.

The necessary basis of an effort to love the truth and abide by its laws is an habitual and courageous exercise of a living faith. To make an act of faith is to surrender to Divine Truth and to expose oneself to the light that comes directly from him. It is to affirm that God is right.

If we have not the sun, how are we going to succeed in recognizing the little glimpses of truth, its poor reflections on things around us? True, the divine sun is overclouded for us in this life, and it is by faith that we see its rays. Yet it is the light and truth of God, and nothing can surpass or supply its benefits to one who has chosen to live by that light, to stay and dwell under it, and bathe in its rays.

"Expose yourselves to the rays of the word of God as a cloth spread out in the sunshine" (St. Margaret Mary). So give yourselves to the gospel that its simple truths penetrate without assistance; keep telling yourselves: this is what is true. Watch our Lord pray, speak, and act and accept all the consequences of his mission. Keep telling yourselves that he was right, for he is God. That is how the truth is bred in us.

Dishonesty, whether deliberate or unintentional, little by little becomes hateful and cries out its own ugliness. Is there not always a trace of it folded away inside us like some counterfeit money that we will not give up?

Attaining through faith a knowledge of divine truth, we begin to learn a love of truth in all its forms.

The truth with oneself

How beautiful a transparent soul is. St. Thérèse of Lisieux said somewhere that the devil cannot bear the pure gaze of a child and runs from it like a coward.

We understand that. But life soon makes us learn the arts of deceit and interior cleverness. Laziness or some passion quickly lead us to discover a thousand ways of avoiding the demands of truth. We fool ourselves more often than we fool others. We dread the sunlight and let dust accumulate on the windows of the soul.

That is why we feel free and joyful when a confession and retreat allow us not only to acknowledge actual sins but also to shake off this torpor and renew our taste for interior truth and candor. That is also why the regular examen is such a rigorous duty and of great benefit to the soul who desires truth and refuses loose and dangerous equivocations.

Everything, even the worst, is possible in a soul which does not sincerely love the light; but nothing is ever lost to one who is unwilling to do without that light.

The truth with others

It is so easy and tempting to get out of a difficulty at the expense of truth! An outright lie, a careful omission, deceit, silence.

A prime example is when we imagine that some impersonal reasons or so-called good intention or the interests of the community call for a lie. And we even entertain the notion that God counsels it.

Another case is when our questioner is not a personal

friend but merely the head of some department or other
sphere of community life and we have some dislike for her;
then the step is quickly taken. No, one does not play with
truth.

Another name for truth is exactitude, however bother-
some it may be. Truth is also precision, and imprecision is
itself a fault and prepares the way for real lies.

One does not play with truth, for we cannot be true to
God if we are not so to our fellows, any more than we can
love him without loving them. It is with God that we are
dealing when we deal with them. *"Thou hast not lied to
men but to God"* (Acts 5, 4). And even though our fellows
are only human beings, we cannot get out of it that way.
When we are false, we lose the simplicity and honesty that
are indispensable to our relations with the God of truth.
This theme is one that merits much reflection. As we have
seen, it reaches into the depths of the soul and extends over
all the surface of life.

We speak of God when we speak of truth. To do the
truth, as our Lord commands (John 3, 21), is difficult but
necessary. To live by faith is the primary and basic preparation and is the measure of our duty.

To be one *"in whom there is no guile"* (John 1, 47) is
a most excellent way of pleasing God.

THE BURDENS OF OTHERS

*"It was our infirmities that he bore, our sufferings that
he endured ..."* (Is. 53, 4). *"Behold the lamb of God, who
takes away the sin of the world"* (John 1, 29). These
divine words are familiar to us and we are not indifferent

to their meaning. Our frequenting of the Eucharistic mysteries keeps us vividly aware of the great reality of the faith: that God took our flesh and humanity upon him. And that throughout his terrible Passion he felt weighing upon him the dreadful burden of man's misery — and thus he saved us.

But it is a long way from our Lord's Passion to our communions, and the mystery contemplated is a far cry from the mystery lived.

Take on the cares of others.

Life keeps forcing them on us in any case. But we accept them as burdens or put up with them as temporary impediments to a liberty that we take for granted. Eventually we will get back to normal. We give service to others without being at their service. We consider those who think otherwise as rather excessive or over-generous. "Fine, let them do as they please, but it's not my way ... the need is real but it's not in my department." We admire them, maybe, but rarely envy them.

We always consider others as more or less intruders when their problems weigh too heavily on us, when their visits become something more than passing ones, or when they cross a certain line that we have drawn and disturb our fastidiously arranged selves. Imagining that our true destiny is to be found in our own inner sanctum, we are willing to make occasional sacrifices to pay for its permanent joys.

It is only too clear that our Lord thought otherwise. He freely and willingly clothed himself in our flesh and our miseries and took them upon himself forever. He was not playing the rôle of man merely for a while: he was and is man. The permanence of his humanity in the divine person is an indication of how we are to view the permanent presence of others in our own lives: a burden not to be laid aside.

Who knows whether an unconscious refusal of this is not the cause of many of our difficulties and deepest problems? When we think we are suffering from the burdens of others, are we not really suffering from our vain efforts to get rid of them? Insofar as we live as Christians, we are as inseparable from others as was Christ. To try to live otherwise is like trying to escape one's shadow. It always follows.

As for Christ, his mission was much more than taking others upon himself. The word used in Holy Scripture signifies both a taking charge and a rescue: he not only relieves our misery but removes it. He is thus presented in the sublime pages of Isaias that we reread every Holy Week, and similarly in the eyes of St. John the Baptist on the bank of the Jordan; both knew him as the Lamb of God.

To take care of others in order to deliver them is the true way, not merely to bear them patiently but to love them and promote their salvation. That is the only way of finding heart enough for a Christian life, for it ties us once and for all to our neighbors.

To bother about them is not to purchase the right to forget them later on. To bother about them is to pay for their salvation in Christ and to assure our own, which will always consist in loving them and make us able one day to share their joy. In other words, it is to share in the life of God who is love and who delights to give.

"To share in the passion of Christ" is neither a quiet personal prayer nor superficial, external devotion to others. It is to carry the weight of mankind on one's back, along with him, and to know that it belongs to all of us. And it is to taste the great joy of cooperation in Christ for the world's salvation.

The burden cannot be lifted, for it is the cross. The carrying of it can never be futile, for the cross saves the world.

May God lead us to accept with all our hearts this "servitude," for it is an honor, joy and the truth.

MUTUAL RESPECT

Under all sorts of forms and expressions — patience, kindness, gentleness, brotherly love — St. Paul reminds us of the duty of politeness in human relations; and in his repeated lessons sets forth the clear and logical demands of love. The marvellous hymn to charity in I Cor. spreads out like a fan the innumerable virtues and infinite demands of charity in the hearts where she reigns.

It is well to examine one's expressions of charity, sometimes humble, sometimes perfunctory, in daily life with our fellows.

True, real charity cannot be uprooted by the shabby ways in which we treat one another now and then. "They love each other after all," people say. Maybe, but charity certainly suffers. And charity is such a great thing — it is God himself — that we dare not use it lightly.

One of the most direct expressions of charity, if it is alive and true, is obviously mutual respect. How can one claim to love what one does not respect?

What then is mutual respect?

First, it is *respect in judgment.*

I refer to mental judgment, before any outward one is expressed (to which we assume we have a right). We seldom exercise it deliberately, but it becomes a natural habit growing out of experience or prejudice. It automatically regulates our conduct and seems an integral part of us, as something innate and private, rather than such a thing as an actual judgment in which we may be wrong.

Someone wrote cruelly but with a certain amount of truth, "We judge most people we know with a simple word — he's a fool, she's impossible." He adds, "I rather think we do not know how to describe those we love."

Where do we get the right to be so high and mighty with those among whom we live? Who has given us the right to pry so unscrupulously into secrets of hearts that belong to God alone? Who authorizes us to analyze and interpret others, to busy ourselves about them, interfere in their affairs, try to bend them in our own ways?

Our actual errors in judgment begin with a lack of interior caution and reserve, allowing us to treat others as pastures where we graze at will. We have no such rights.

You may say, "My intentions are not evil or uncharitable."

And I would reply with a simple question, "What would they think, who are the subjects of your inner thoughts?" They have a right to our inner respect. They would have it if our love were pure enough.

Another form of respect is *discretion*.

A respect for human rights should keep us from burdening others with troubles or annoyances. We have received an order to shoulder the burdens of others, but not an invitation to impose ours on *them*.

To share troubles and cares when necessary is to carry them more easily. To shoulder everything indiscriminately is to increase the weight on ourselves and to run the risk of forgetting our chief and most powerful support: he who asks us to carry his burden that he may take ours, and to carry the cross in his steps.

There is a lack of respect for others in wanting them to be constantly concerned about ourselves. There are many things about us that can well be left unsaid; speaking of them not only hardens them but makes others' burdens seem unduly heavy. Our real confidant should be he who alone helps and heals.

Indiscreet confidences that impose our cares on others are a counterpart of the indiscretion that lets the uninvited ideas of others penetrate into our spirits. We know well that such lack of respect is contrary to true charity: no one gains, neither God nor others nor ourselves.

Divine charity is the source of mutual respect.

The only way of achieving this respect, of appreciating how much we owe it, and of gaining the strength for it, is to grow in charity — or rather to ask the author of charity to make it grow in us.

To respect others is not to be distant, but the contrary: it calls for a deepening of our esteem and of the most discreet attention possible. Treat them as God treats you: with this ideal, all poor excuses are swept away. And in the end it is easier to love when we let charity have its own wonderful way. Our Lord himself lets us know that and gives us the grace for it.

OBEDIENCE

Poverty entails some sacrifices and a general vigilance, but we accept it with little difficulty. Chastity presents its trials, but we keep this vow too with a certain watchfulness against indelicacy and it is no great burden. Obedience is something else. Obedience is the greatest self-sacrifice and the definitely indisputable sign of faithfulness: renunciation of self for the Other. It is the ultimate test of love. Do you really love God more than yourself? Obedience is the only answer.

Therefore we must cultivate it with the greatest care, as if it were a rare and tender flower which costs us much but whose perfume is pleasing to God.

Giving up what one has is nothing compared to giving up oneself. Obedience can only be understood as the supreme flowering of love. It is both bitter and sweet: sweet because of the love that causes and inspires it, bitter because of the self-immolation involved.

Jesus died in obedience. One may say equally that he died for love. But the obedience in which his love was rooted and which gave him reason to spend himself, supplanted that love with pain.

Love which does not obey is questionable. Love which does obey mingles tears with enduring, mysterious joy. When one understands the importance of obedience, it is not astonishing that it costs so dearly. Therefore we ought to try to exercise it as sincerely and perfectly as possible, to amass a great treasure.

We are generally apt to cultivate other virtues, for they develop more easily.

As for obedience, we feel well enough off when we do not fail in it or commit a sin of omission. We fear more than we love.

Certainly obedience is not amiable in the mere human sense of the word; but it can be so in a loftier sense, insofar as our attitude is pleasing to him whom we love. From this point of view, it is truly amiable, worth all our efforts, and a source of special joy.

Obedience is not something we *submit*: it is a proof of love or it is nothing. It is something we sincerely wish. Because it pleases God, we make an effort to perfect our obedience by ridding it of anything that would undermine it, and of any withholding, resistance, or refusal.

True obedience is not at all passive; love is not passive, and love and inertia are incompatible. Nothing resembles obedience less than indifference or automatism, for love knows nothing of such things.

And that is why the spiritual demands of obedience are basically at one with those of authority. What is the exercise of authority if it is not a humble abandonment to divine providence? It is not suprising that, the higher one is placed, the greater humility God demands. It is an essential need, not a matter of prudence or policy.

It is love that makes the good Superior, a love for God and his will — not for her position or for a Rule as such — and for her sisters as beloved of God.

This same love makes obedient sisters, a love of God and his will — of which the Superior is the instrument — and love for superiors as beloved of God.

If we understand this all the differences to which we are so naturally sensitive end by disappearing in a higher unity.

What is it to order?

What is it to obey?

Is it not to love God and one another in the situations in which he places us in this body which is himself, fashioned with his own hands?

May God help us to understand it.

BLESSED ARE THE POOR

Poverty is one of the Beatitudes of the Gospel, and indeed it is the first. It is one of the essential conditions that God asks of those he loves, and one they spontaneously offer.

Poverty joyously accepted in the spirit of a religious vocation is indeed a beatitude. Those who have truly and willingly agreed to it are never let down as "they live from day to day," in the wonderful words of Bernanos, "and feed from the hand of God." St. Francis is but the type of thousands and thousands of others in the Church for whom poverty — according to this world — has been a synonym of joy.

Poverty has never been a disappointment to those who live by it in answer to our Lord's call. The poor make discoveries each day — more discoveries than new efforts. The constantly recurring necessity of turning to God, the ever-present chances of seeing his face, make the children of God like "the birds of the air" in their lightness and freedom. But this supposes that one experiences poverty. Only through need does poverty produce its fruit of hope — and joy, which is the fruit of hope. The one who has "possessions" and is "secure" is not poor, and what he has is a meager substitute for the direct reliance on God which is the privilege of the poor.

"Blessed are the poor," but, to recall the words of the ancient Latin poet, "only when they realize their advantage."

Poverty can be nothing but a more or less painful sacrifice which we stave off or cope with as best we can. It can be something withstood without any of the abandon or risks that make it worth the price.

The vow of poverty is not worth making and becomes unprofitable and meaningless, unless it is lived.

Remember that we have the Church's experience to direct us in the way of poverty. The Church knows that all sorts of fantasies and ventures have been made in the name of poverty, and have made their victims too. Sometimes they have borne good fruit and been worthwhile — if redeemed only by poverty itself.

It is not a question of looking over the wall at living conditions of utter poverty, perhaps even poorer than ours, for God has not called us to that. Let us look at ourselves and the life around and before us.

There is no lack of opportunity to live the vow of *real* poverty even in a community which has no apparent reason to worry about tomorrow's needs.

A community might sometimes be tempted to "seek security" in a measure beyond the prudent requirements of the Church or what the constitutions allow, with the excuse that there are so many demands on it that this is necessary. However, more often than not these are just excuses.

A nun might be personally "secure" beyond the requirements of the community, of her daily life and work. She might feel secure through attachment to all sorts of personal things to which she clings or which tie others to her. She might even feel secure against having to give an account and even against the necessity of turning to God and abandoning herself in him.

This is a false security!

Poverty is a beatitude.

Blessed is she who experiences it.

At the summit of perfection we find a St. Francis, who

merits our reflections: a poor man, truly poor, poor as Christ.

In our times, whoever loves the Church must think carefully of poverty: for the world needs it as an example of faith.

Who will set the example if not you?

Are you doing it?

Pay no attention to what the world thinks of you, for it is insignificant. It only must grasp that you are *"as having nothing yet possessing all things"* (II Cor. 6, 10). People must see that they belong to you as they did to St. Francis. All poor men, the truly poor, belong. The world belongs to no one as it does to the poor. Things are not as they are except by the God who made them. They are related to the Lord and whatever beauty and existence they have is his reflection. He has not carelessly tossed people into space and left them there: they are constantly drawn to him and receive from him reasons for existence.

Francis sees and knows them; he immediately falls in love with them and they belong to him; yet at the same time he can, so to speak, step aside and watch them turning in the hands of the divine potter and being endowed with his gifts.

That is Francis.

He does not begin his canticle with "Praised be the sun," but with "Praised be the Lord for our brother the sun. . . ."

Now let me speak once more about the matter of being truly poor and in particular about not loving money. St. Francis loved so many things, but detested money; "excrement of the devil," he called it.

Money is not of God's making but is the sign of human ownership. It is the token of possession of a possibly deadly promise of profane pleasures and an enticement from true happiness in Christ. Money as a sign of human ownership detaches the things of God from him who gave them being; and as a symbol of human pleasure, it attaches men to other things than their God. Money contributes to our forgetfulness of God and finally brings us to the un-happy proposition, "You must choose between God and mammon."

St. Francis scented these dangers, the most serious risks that a man can run. Creatures are so beautiful as they are, fashioned by the hand of God and gravitating toward him. What a joy to be poor and share such richness.

COVETOUSNESS, WHICH IS IDOLATRY

We are generally on our guard against many dangers that can disrupt our union with God and risk *"grieving the Holy Spirit"* (Eph. 4, 30).

The lusts of the flesh in particular are strong but they immediately arouse our consciences. We know by instinct how far we can be carried, and there is always an instant when we can cast off the illusion — even after it is too late. It is not the same with the cunningly insidious enemy against which long human experience and divine warnings in Holy Scripture speak: *this enemy is money.*

The Church, enlightened and animated by the Holy Spirit, immediately recognized the danger, and those who sought after God with all their hearts and were willing to take giant steps to do so, decided to shake off any slavery to money. Poverty was from the start and has been ever since one of the features of every ideal of Christian perfection.

But each one must keep his own conscience perpetually alert to the dangers that threaten it day after day. In myriad forms, dressed in unsuspected and attractive garb, the enemy returns. There is nothing to arouse a sense of menace; on the contrary, a thousand reasons seem to support money's cause and turn good will into an accomplice. So if it is true that one must be constantly on guard against the flesh and its pleasures, how much more sternly and severely alert to the temptations of money must we be.

We can be fooled in so many ways.

We can be fooled as individuals no matter what our profession or loyalties may be. One cannot forget the thirty insulting pieces of silver for which Judas betrayed his master. We are often apt to betray him for much less.

"It is a small thing," we are used to saying in respect to little things we must do without. But even our indifference is threatened: it grows on us even at prayer or work until the small thing we lack becomes more necessary than the really important ones. The threat is shown in the trouble we have in getting rid of these distractions even briefly: we *must* have it or we cannot go on.

Is this not a chain? a slavery?

And who can describe all the pettiness and compromise of which we become capable once we give ourselves to such longings? We leave behind peace of mind, self-respect, often candor and honesty; we sacrifice friendship and obedience. *"All these things will I give thee"* (Matt. 4, 9). That is one of Christ's temptations recorded in the gospel and is the devil's usual approach. What good is "freedom in Christ" if we are enslaved in this way? Desires which we neither can nor will admit, secret attachments to worthless things, are as a clandestine marriage when we have already willingly renounced worldly good fortune for God.

However even when we have mastered these temptations in their interior and personal aspects, it happens that they recur in a collective way. A community whose members have individually accepted the ideal of poverty can collectively acquire a taste for wealth. This is one of the maneuvers of which the devil is a past master. Victories gained in the field of poverty and sacrifices accepted by individuals end by being the means of a communal defeat. The devil has regained everything at no cost and has re-entered by a back door. It is the winning point in slyness and trickery.

Insofar as the individual conscience finds no cause for self-accusation, it can be readily strict and rigorous. In truth we are unaware that we have a love for money; yet we are its servants, for we save it, watch over it, accumulate it. Money ceases to dominate individuals only to become the tyrant of all (cf. Eph. 5, 5).

The demands of a rule or the ordinances of the Church are no protection in this case, it seems. The Church wants superiors and others in responsibility to be mindful of the welfare of those in their charge; but this does not mean that the Church allows to communities what she forbids to its individual members. We all know what the ideal of poverty is. It is just as possible on the collective level as it is on the individual.

Be ready to give. Be ready to give generously. Prefer what is moderate. Limit provisions to what are necessities. Help one another. Strictly reject any dealings that seem "interesting." Avoid the notion that individual poverty is accommodated by the management of communal weath.

Innumerable mottoes of that sort seek to prevent evils and give not only individuals but communities the freedom and divine abandonment in which the world can recognize the presence and action of God.

The devil has devised nothing more detestable than money to degrade mankind, draw us away from God, and rob us of the benefits of our highest efforts. This needs to be said and understood and we must be on guard.

The more need the world has of the witness of poverty, the more those who are so vowed must take care not to lose the fruits of their vocation.

"Blessed are the poor!" is our Lord's promise.

RELIGIOUS DEMEANOR

People of our day mistrust formality, and everything that is conventional and customary is under suspicion. They name it conformity and think and even say that it is hypocrisy. "Sincerity" and "authenticity" hold sway. The religious life does not escape this liberally reforming trend, and a great broom of simplicity is brushing away dusty old traditions or else making them seem ridiculous.

Should we then cast aside "religious demeanor," which has always been part of our tradition, as a sort of handmaid employed by love as an aid to perfection? We ought to think very carefully before dispensing with this modest sister who is in charge of the manners and looks of the house.

It is commonly said that we do not need stiffness.

We certainly do not: far from stiffness, we need the suppleness and adaptability that are the basis of respect for

3 *The Nun:*

others. Even if it takes a great deal of effort, we must learn to treat others with due respect to their age, sex, and situation in life. This is one way of realizing that they are persons, not things. Pascal said, "Respect means to inconvenience yourself." All sorts of good manners are required of us in life's various relationships: of the child toward its parents, of all of us in respect to the elderly, of a man toward a woman, of a woman toward a man, of the inferior in the presence of a superior.

There is no reasonable excuse for doing away with formalities. Although they can be exaggerated and insincere, they can be inordinately stiff, yet at their best they maintain irreplaceable values. We lose the value when we give up its normal expression, and our Lord's words apply here, "Do this but do not leave the other undone."

Mutual respect among mankind is demonstrated in very simple ways: formality and gesture, manner and tone. Yes, they are all conventional, but conventions are better than nothing, and a lack of formality suggests unfriendliness.

Simple decency obviously enters into this matter of respect for others. There are careless people who say it does not matter; but there is reason to be wary of them and not let ourselves be fooled. Laxity is always distinguishable from simplicity.

It is easy to see where charity belongs in this sphere: charity pushes us to every and any limit of Christian life and fellowship, and nothing — not even negligence in demeanor — is out of the realm of the Gospel.

Of course this is a superficial matter and there is a tendency to prejudice about it. Vanity does cause people to spend much time over their toilettes and appearances, but that does not mean that they have no proper place in life.

St. Francis de Sales always dressed very simply, but in purple, which was not cheap!

Some of the best ways to exercise humility are in matters of appearances: one can be pleasing, unassuming, and real. A certain community has "uniformity" written into its rule, and our first reaction is one of dismay; but soon we see that the discarding of a personal *singularity* makes for marvellous distinctions of spirit.

For a world so disconcerted in this and other ways, what better lesson is there than the traditional religious demeanor? What greater blessing to the face of life than the shining out of this interior gift which is real freedom? What catastrophes for herself and others await the "freeswinging personality" who spurns the wisdom of Christian experience, for it is really an abandonment of peace of mind. A lack of self-possession and proper demeanor invite the attacks of the world.

Real freedom has been given us by Christ at great cost; it binds us to him, liberates us from sin, and makes us servants of justice. Divine enlightenment about the importance of little things like manners is in itself a great grace.

PURITY OF INTENTION

It is not healthy to be constantly watching oneself or exercising a perpetually rigorous self-analysis and examen. God loves us too much for that sort of thing to be his will.

To do what the Church has learned by experience and written into religious rules is enough: careful self-examination daily, and careful, simple, and confident preparation for confession.

However we must keep desiring and cultivating what is usually called "purity of intention," for we have there our greatest means of holding on to and using the gifts of grace.

What is purity of intention?

Everyone must have found some interpretation of the words, whether by real experience or by regarding it as a great goal. There is a hidden place in each of us that waits to be uncovered. At one time or another we grow aware of it and find it a reservoir of peace, light, clarity, and truth; and once we realize its existence, we never forget or doubt that it is always there. It is the place where the soul says Yes to God. Simply Yes, nothing more, neither of qualifications nor emotions. The simple Yes is the clearest reply but is not therefore a limited one.

To be fair, the discovery of some point in our hearts where God's will and our own are joined and united is never a mere accident it is there because we are willing and able to support it. Purity of intention is found there: it dwells in that part of the soul which at one time or another has known the unspeakable joy of saying Yes to God. Recall and return to it so that one day it may become not a part of us but our entire selves.

It was thus with the Blessed Virgin, the Immaculate one.

But the paths that lead us to this spot are constantly cluttered with the complications of life and the pressures of the world. They are often so obstructed that we cannot find them again. For the assurance of pure intention and a life centred around this core of which we have been speaking, we must take on wholeheartedly the simple if tiresome jobs of highway maintenance crews, so to speak. They keep the roads open, see that the signs are properly posted, clear away the trash and fallen branches, and keep the highways ready at all times for normal traffic. The roads are the same for everyone and are marked with the signs of primary, everyday virtues: patience, faithfulness in prayer, self-dedication, humility, devotion to duty. Yet each of us has his special street, for certain virtues are more prominent in one than in another. Those that are more easily travelled by some may seem obscure to others.

Each nun must, so to speak, plan her own interior road map. She will quickly see the shortcuts, steep or difficult though they may be, to reach her destination, and also see the treacherous spots, as on a mountain road in winter. She will watch out for fallen rocks and unexpected ditches and pot-holes, for it is generally the little things that clog our interior paths, as fallen snow blocks the highways. She will admit to stupid and inglorious failings yet not let weakness undermine her courage or vanity and jealously gnaw silently at her heart.

The game is worth the trouble. For its prize, one appreciates little by little the countless joys in calling God our Father, in living in communion with Christ and in complete accord with our Lady.

You know that no worldly joys are comparable. Why hesitate then at what God offers you?

PURITY OF HEART

The Church wishes all her people to make constant efforts to be pure in heart — gently, quietly but tirelessly. In the religious life, such efforts and the quality of our perseverance will come within the framework of regular and frequent confession and the grace of absolution.

Fortunately Lent renews our appreciation of this sacrament and our sense of its need. It is a sacrament: which is to say that it is primarily a divine grace rather than an occasion for spiritual exercise. Think of it as a heavenly gift rather than a human effort. In the sacrament of Penance all the wonderful benefits of the Passion of our Lord that we need or can grasp are poured out upon us. We tend to think of ourselves as the principal actors in this sacrament, when it is God who has the chief role. In Holy Week, aside from the Paschal Communion itself, there is no better way to the loving heart of our Lord than this sacrament.

What a wonderful Lent it would be if we all ended it with a new understanding and fresh appreciation of regular confession.

States of mind vary greatly in approaching the sacrament of Penance. It is always possible to grow negligent and go to confession only at overlong intervals, or to prepare without sufficient strictness or seriousness. One can let confessions degenerate into mere twaddle to which God is superfluous; or turn them into a uselessly harsh self-accusation on the one hand, or a complacent self-appraisal on the other. God can get lost in our confessions and so can our sins!

One comes to dread going to confession. At least one does not like it. But confession is beloved and precious to those who see there the face of our Lord, a face never more beautiful than when he forgives, aglow with contagious joy as he finds occasion to confer his grace.

How can we rediscover this means of grace buried under so many senseless habits?

There is one thing in a religious which neither time nor neglect can effect: the love our Lord has given her. Whatever may have happened, the love remains and distinguishes her from all others in the eyes of her Spouse. On God's part, this love never dies; nor does it in the human partner. In fact to say that God loves us is quite one and the same thing as saying that he makes us able to love him. In calling anyone to a life of perfection, God endows her with ways of loving only him and never withdraws them. With this in mind, every religious can feel that Christ is indispensable and sufficient, and wish him to remain so. And beginning there, she will recover the infinite sweetness and assurance of the sacrament of Penance.

Suffer for having been displeasing

Suffer because you are no longer what Jesus wanted you to be. That is how a religious ought to understand sin.

For Christ has chosen a spouse and given himself to her in all the intimacy that the words imply; and she is a spouse whose only rule must be to be pleasing to her husband. These are not the words of a sentimentalist but of St. Paul (I Cor. 7, 32 ff). And we on earth know also that we must think of pleasing a spouse crucified: by sharing in his offering.

"I do not wish to store up merits: I want to work only to give pleasure to Jesus," says St. Theresa in her act of offering. Blessed is the religious who learns in Lent that the best synonym for sin is "that which displeases Jesus." Then contrition will grow in a natural way and achieve the perfection of which the catechism speaks and which merges into charity.

Why not? Besides, what other way is there?

Delight in pleasing Jesus

There is no pride here. He who clothed us in the wedding garments which are in fact himself (for "we have put on Christ," Gal. 3, 27), he is the one who makes us worthy of his glance. Our beauty is his work. Faith teaches us that he himself acts and accomplishes this work through the sacrament of Penance.

A religious who knows herself loved by God and suffers in displeasing him and comes from the confessional to the glory of Easter morning can rejoice in the certainty that she is pleasing to our Lord and that he delights in loving her. She can well appreciate the meaning of our Lord's words recorded in Matthew 19, 12.

There is unique paschal joy promised to the religious who believes in her espousal and has spent a good Lent in relearning the meaning of sin and forgiveness.

There is the unique joy of offering our Lord what he expects of the souls he has chosen, and the very thought of it can inspire wonderful generosity.

"To be loved and to love" is how St. Theresa described her vocation and aspiration, and it is in fact the destiny and wish of a spouse. A renewal of penitence stirs up these convictions in us, and the whole Church will benefit: for to be loved and to love demands a will to "make love."

SIN

Lately one has been hearing talk of "the sins of society." The phrase's currency is a response to a need to express a sense of interdependence and the existence of common and diffuse responsibilities; it also expresses a common guilt for the outrages of life — the injustices, the unfair inequalities, the sufferings calmly ignored or condoned. However, this rude awakening of the social conscience has unfortunately taken a wrong turn — or risks doing so — in gradually hushing the *individual conscience.*

It is precisely in the heart of the individual person that the word sin takes on its meaning. It is in the direct confrontation of God and a man with his free will that the Yes or No is spoken and where sin is consummated in a mysterious spiritual disorder, in disobedience to the divine law, in turning away from God. This disobedience is reparable only by the perfect obedience of the Word made flesh.

Definitely and essentially sin is a refusal to love. It is meaningless except in the heart, where love ebbs and flows.

More than ever, a nun must keep within her a feeling of horror of sin. She owes it to God and she owes it to the world of today, where the sense of sin is dying out.

This requires that we will not let the meaning of sin be altered. In all theological definition and truth, sin is primarily, essentially, and always the refusal to love. The first epistle of St. John tells us this over and over. Mortal sin is the deliberate and direct refusal and repudiation of love. That is why any sin against charity in which the soul is engaged with full knowledge and consent cannot but be mortal.

Let me say here that I am not speaking of love in terms of sentiments or inclinations of the heart, but in terms of free acceptance of the will of God. To will what God wills in his good pleasure, to wish to please him, is the only true love; and sin is always some sort of rejection of that attitude. This does not mean that sin does not take many forms and find varied occasions: indeed that divine will that we are bound to love — for it is God himself — is expressed serially, not all at once but by particular orders.

His orders are the virtues that he wishes to see in us, those that delineate our vocations and destinies and that will gradually transform us into his image the molds that he makes for us. Has not God *"created man in his image"* (Gen. 1, 27), conforming him also to the likeness of his own Son, the firstborn of all creation (Col. 1, 15)? To him must we keep our *"faces unveiled, reflecting as in a mirror the glory of the Lord ... transformed into his very image from glory to glory"* (II Cor. 3, 18).

The divine will in general or in particular is brought to us in the form of commandments: universal commandments expressing the divine law as man has grasped it and as interpreted and established by the Church, and by particular commandments which relate the universal ones to our daily lives. How firmly our Lord spoke of his Father's will throughout the Last Supper: *"I do as the Father has commanded me — arise, let us go."* And on the cross, *"It is consummated"* marks the satisfaction of one who has finished his work with love and obedience to the end.

When we think of the nature of sin along these lines, two things are clear: the thought of sin ought to inspire dread yet it ought never to lead to scrupulosity!

Sin is never anything but the refusal of love to the God of infinite love; its work in the soul is repulsive. How is it possible that we so often affront the will of God who wishes us happiness without ever exerting his absolute claim on us except to rescue us and to give himself to us in communion?

We know that Jesus has had to suffer much in reparation for this insult and offense. We know too that God has true friends who, unable to let him suffer alone, have become wholehearted collaborators in the work of Christ for the salvation of their brethren and for the glory of God. But scrupulosity itself can arise only from a misunderstanding of the nature of sin. The one way to conquer sin, which is a refusal of love, is to love more fully. The one and only way to make reparation is to love more.

Scrupulosity can exist only when we see sin with a warped vision or so lose ourselves in its details that we cannot see the wood for the trees. We miss the fact that the one way to forgiveness is to love more. Scrupulosity is a mistake and does harm through sheer waste; it goes against truth and ultimately impedes the freedom sought by grace. The first way of fighting against it and preventing it is to have a strong and right sense of sin. When we are tempted, a firm purpose and obedience to what we have learned by experience will make up for our weakness and lead us to light.

We are no longer servants of the law, but children of God (Rom. 8, 15).

Sin must horrify us if we love God and know that it offends him. Our reaction to our own sins must only be to love more. Our only reaction to the sins of others, far from disdaining them, must be to love them more, so that redeeming grace may lead them back to the Father and his love.

In this sphere perhaps more than in any other, a right vision is the condition of doing well.

Bring yourself to say with your heart the simple prayer our Lord taught us: "Father . . . thy will be done."

HATRED OF SIN

Sin!

It is a commonplace to say that the world around us is losing all sense of that word, just as it is losing knowledge of God and his laws, of which sin is the contradiction.

Therefore we must arm ourselves more than ever against a danger which cannot but affect us.

Is *our* sense of sin real and alive? Does sin really make us suffer? Is it a real incentive to acts of reparation which will also be redemptive ones?

Of course sin makes us suffer.

Whether they be our own sins or others'.

Whether they be the sins that the world shamelessly displays in all possible forms.

But not all such pangs of conscience about our sins or those of the world are necessarily sound: Judas too repented, and we should take warning.

There is a way, or rather there are ways of being remorseful which can be bad and even positively unhealthy. We can readily feel humiliated for our sins, but if the regrets are rooted only in pride, they amount to no more than an expression of self-love. It will not be a pain that ends in healing, but one evil added to another: the mortally sick sadness of which St. Paul speaks in II Cor. 7, 10.

We can be weighed down by our sins and let them overcome us. A sadness for sin which contains no hope cannot be of God, for it leads us to be dismayed and to give up. Remember the prophecy, *"J take no pleasure in the death of the wicked man, but rather in the wicked man's conversion, that he may live"* (Ez. 33, 11). God does not demand abject sorrow.

Nor is it called for in respect to the sins of others. One is suspicious of indignation as a form of hostility to evil, for it can be but a ready and easy way of advertizing one's own virtuous feelings. Indignation costs nothing and produces nothing; it spends itself in words, makes others discouraged, and accomplishes no good. It all seems to be too much on a natural level, whether it is merely instinctive or whether it is unconsciously calculated, which is no better. That is not the way to despise evil if one loves God.

This brings us to the heart of the matter: the love of God and hatred of sin are two sides of the same coin.

Sin is a contradiction of all that the law sums up as implicit in love for God and our brethren. Ultimately therefore, to hate sin means to be unable to admit or allow that God go unloved or that men love not one another. That sort of impatience alone is holy.

All the particular prescriptions of the law and its demands for divers virtues are but varied expressions of what is implicit in the precept of charity. It is charity that gives each of us a soul and is the original author of the divine law. Therefore any Christian virtue must be a lifeless thing without the love of God.

At the bottom of all hatred for sin there must exist a charity which will not be overriden nor let itself be silenced. When hatred for sin is real and true it will manifest such traits of charity as St. Paul described in his first epistle to the Corinthians. Charity must indeed be a burning thing, for it is another name for love, and love is a flame; but it must be a flame that gives warmth and light, not one that destroys. Be zealous to overcome evil *"but overcome evil with good"* (Rom 12, 21).

Never be lax or timid to condemn sin.

Never be motivated or guided by anything but the hope of forwarding the triumph of good in the souls even of those who are fighting against it. One is always moved in recalling the words of St. Augustine, which he attributes to the divine voice: "You ask for the death of the sinner.... Which one of the two?".

This means that our duty today more than ever is boldly to recognize evil for what it is, whether that around us or that within us.

To love God is to say, Thy will be done. He wills that his name be known, honored, and hallowed; he wills that his wonderful work for the salvation of the world be known and proclaimed to men freely and loudly; he wills that self-respect and mutual respect, without which love is only a word, may prevail among men.

If we love God, we must often suffer bitterly because of the world's deaf ears and its lack of response to God or his laws and promises. *A fortiori* we suffer because of the insults the world so proudly offers him; we suffer too because of the widespread immorality and the prevalent civil injustices condoned by law. On earth, one who loves God cannot be happy in the human sense of the word: the ineffable joy of loving God is combined with a deep knowledge of the sufferings of the Redeemer.

We must also suffer from loving God enough to accomplish his will to perfection, and from the fact that we are sinners. However we can be sure that such suffering, when it is sincere and humbly confident, is a way of loving. It will encourage us to untiring efforts to pick ourselves up and start off afresh. From one failure to another we still move toward God. It is our love that God will judge.

This love is not real if it is not also a hatred for sin. It must be so, for the first epistle of St. John leaves us no alternative.

May the risen Lord pour into our hearts the fire of his Holy Spirit and may it shine upon us like the flames that enkindled his disciples at Pentecost.

THE CONSCIENCE AND HATRED OF SIN

The world's growing indifference to sin — in other words, to God — is a painful fact. Indifference to sin is a sign, an effect, and at the same time a cause of indifference to God.

When sin has hardly any meaning and no longer evokes any reaction or revulsion, it is because God is scarcely known or loved. A sense and fear of sin indicate awareness of the presence of God and their disappearance is a sign of his absence. God grows more and more distant as the conscience dies and feelings grow cold.

A religious ought to estimate the seriousness and widespread nature of this sickness, to consider the possibility of contagion, and to offer to our Lord her best efforts for those in danger.

The evil that causes this sickness is deep. Let us try to see its dimensions.

There have always been and always will be the offenses of the world; until the end, Christ will be in agony and will offer his sacrifice for the remission of sins.

We know that we all contribute to the sins of the world and all have need of redemption. Each of us knows by experience that the devil is at work; each time we are caught off guard, it is a victory for the enemy; each of us knows that we sin seven times a day and must sincerely admit it. One cannot say the Hail Mary without being willingly included among "us sinners." One cannot say the Our Father without acknowledging trespasses that need forgiveness.

The first step in prayer therefore must be an arousing of conscience to the fact of one's sinfulness, together with a humble gratitude for the unmerited grace that leads us to appreciate that fact.

Evil flows around us and its waters, polluted with sins of flesh and spirit, are constantly splashing over us; and what is most alarming is the growing indifference on the part of those who are stained.

"They do not know what they are doing" (Luke 23, 34).

In his agonized yet sublime prayer, he who dies upon the cross says enough to underline for us the fatal unawareness of so many men. They no longer look to God nor do they know how to seek him in their inmost selves where he dwells; so they are unable to compare themselves with him in whose image they are made, much less to realize that they are disfigured.

God alone knows the heart's secrets; he alone is man's judge and he jealously reserves this right. Yet we cannot remain heedless of man's indifference to his divine destiny and the loss that he risks.

Wherever evil manifests itself, it is important that it arouse in us disgust, dread, and hatred as strong as our love for God, who is offended, and for our brethren who are losing their souls. For there *is* somthing we can do.

We are not mere spectators, much less censors. We are associates of him who has conquered sin and we have at our disposal the same forces which were, in him, victorious. Make no mistake: this power is love.

The absence of love accounts for all sin and for the indifference that is worse than sin. We do not conquer evil by evil, "we overcome evil with good."

To counter the world's progressive apathy to sin and its insensibility to the divine will, it is in our power to pour out upon the world more and more real charity. Charity will arouse the drowsing consciences and even resurrect the dead by showing them signs of the true image of God. Charity will finally make the world know what sin is.

They no longer recognize sin because they no longer have a vision of God; but they will recognize it when they have seen God in the persons of those who bear his sign on their foreheads and who desire to live in Christ. When they have seen and believed in love, which is the name of God, it will come home to them with a shock that they have not loved, and then they will be saved.

There is your direction; there is no other way. He who is called Jesus has shown us this way; he walks before us and keeps pointing out the route. It is by *"reflecting as in a mirror the glory of the Lord"* (II Cor. 3, 18) that our own true faces are revealed.

Moreover we know that he who leads us carries his cross and that his followers must take up their own. When you are dismayed by some burden to be endured, remember St. Paul's words to his disciples, *"You have not yet resisted unto blood in the struggle with sin"* (Heb. 12, 4).

The sins of the world are to be regarded neither with curiosity nor mere disgust, much less indignation. One can and must approach them only with our Redeemer, suffering with him for the healing of the world.

Pray that the world may recover a sense of sin and a hatred for it, that men may lose their burden of guilt and be renewed by love — which consists in meekly *"living according to the commandments"* (II John 6). Day by day shoulder the burden of this love, which is Christ's, who saves the world by his cross.

SELF-POSSESSION

Modern science has considerable means of reaching the soul through the body. There are more and more specialists for our nervous systems, which govern both our bodies and our spirits. The separation between the realm of emotion and that of conscience becomes ever more vague and it is a very short step from neurology to psychiatry; and medical practice in these fields is on the increase.

The remedies, too, increase. People talk glibly of sedatives and tranquillizers, and one reads the statistics of the amounts consumed — tons of them in a single year in our country alone. It is not astonishing to see new illnesses arising in the places of the old ones that have been conquered, and the new illnesses have given rise to new remedies used inordinately and without control.

It is a sign of our times, this foolish answer to a need born of a society that moves too fast, is overexcited, tense, and ceaselessly impelled by new stimulants; it is a society incapable of recovering or adopting the prudent rhythms of tension and release, silence and speech, action and recollection. Yet it is clear that there is something serious about this need which men seek rather to satisfy than to control, something serious about the remedies devised more for repairing its ravages than for curbing its demands — and which in fact end by aggravating the maladies.

What am I driving at?

It is by no means certain that the maladies will stop short of our religious communities, and this calls for new attention to spiritual care and discipline and a solid effort to acquire those virtues more than ever necessary in the face of the present dangers. For after all, it is not only the nun herself who is involved in the world, but also her Master; for his name's sake she owes it to the world to be his example.

Is she setting that example in spiritual balance and self-possession? If not, let her examine herself, be vigilant, and take the necessary means. God asks it of her and the Church needs it.

You may ask, What is to be done? This is what life has become. There is no denying that, and a longing for the tranquillity of yesterday is useless. What our real duty is is to face the facts and not allow this new way of life to ruin for us the conditions for human and Christian living. And it is an even stronger duty to acquire and reinforce fixed spiritual habits, a religion that is imperturbable. To be lacking in this is truly sinful, and we are doubly guilty if we have charge of others.

If the conditions of life are new, then we must find ways to accommodate ourselves to them without damage to the spirit. If we do not do so, we are apt to find ourselves carried away by the currents of the times and, when prayer becomes difficult, tempted to replace it with activity. A new energy must be brought to our efforts, whether in connection with ways that used to be taken for granted and were more or less automatic, or in finding new ways.

Self-possession remains a virtue. It is no more dispensable

than chastity. It must astonish us that, being a virtue, it costs us much.

Is it possible to be explicit about one or another of these directions of spiritual pursuits, when the calls of grace clash with the disordered rhythms of life, and the prevalent anxieties and nervousness produce a sickening fluctuation between spiritual exaltation and sudden depressions?

There are indeed those temperamentally and sometimes incurably inclined to live in a state of ups and downs; and the nature of religious vocation demands that superiors discern and assess manic-depressive characters. However, no one can escape a training that often seems rough and wrenching, for everywhere and in everyone are found the dangers of a lack of balance, of instability, of the tyranny of moods, all of them aggravated by life as it is today. Moreover the benefits of even the best training will be lost if it is not tightly interlaced with exact and firm discipline.

Here are some examples of simple principles to be maintained without hesitation:

Sleep is a duty: undisturbed and adequate sleep is a necessity and she who sacrifices it is wrong. Superiors who do not heed this or guarantee it in the assignment of duties are also guilty.

Regular rest periods, vacations in one form or another, are indispensable; and real repose is not to be confused with a mere respite from daily tasks on the one hand nor the exercises of a retreat on the other.

When we come to see the results of negligence in this sphere, it is often too late, and we find the maladies already developed.

The spiritual work of self-mastery and emotional control, despite the means and methods so beautifully analyzed by St. Francis de Sales in his *Introduction to the Devout Life* and other works and letters, is impossible without the proper physical preliminaries.

A peaceful soul, a serene countenance, a stable character are a great blessing in the epoch in which we live — a blessing not only to the possessor but to all around her. She is a true light in a world where everything is changing.

The religious has these graces; she must know how to use them and be ready to find the best means to do so.

THE SOUL, A "MISSIONARY LAND"?

Yes, if God were to disappear!

What if his image were to fade away before our eyes?

Is this a bad dream? For large parts of the world it is a reality. The youthful troops who parade down Moscow's broad avenues no longer know what the bulbous domes and golden gables stood for . . . religion is only a word to them, or a childish and dangerous superstition.

And what can be said of China? Let God disappear. This terrifying prospect makes one shudder.

It is reassuring to think that God will always remain within men's hearts and souls. Even in those countries where there has been a concerted effort to uproot and wipe out every trace of his presence, it is evident that he remains; the continuing efforts are themselves a witness to the failure to drive him out.

It may very well be that these caves of refuge in men's hearts offer, in the face of catastrophe, God's place of "survival" amongst us. For that very reason, let us explore the capacity of such inner refuges and ask ourselves whether God is as really present there as we like to think.

If he disappeared externally, are we so sure that he would be really and completely present internally?

We talk much of missions.

We think of large parts of the world, far and near, which remain to be won to God. Beside foreign missions there are urgent ones right here at home, so that one may speak of "exterior" and "interior" missions.

Let us think also of the most interior and intimate of missions, viz., that which operates within each of us. The Spirit of God extends not only across the time and space of the world: he penetrates each individual with his vibrant flame.

Each of us is a missionary territory comprising zones not yet won to God or else lost and waiting to be rewon. How many sectors and recesses there are in us comparable on the one hand to virgin forests, on the other to the de-Christianized regions of which one hears so much, or to those falsely converted, of the sort spotlighted by Catholic Action.

If God were to seek refuge within us, he would not always find a ready place.

Against the day that men drive God out of the visible world — insofar as they would be able to do so — we must prepare him an inner refuge from which he can return refreshed to the battle.

So we must explore ourselves and draw up a map, as it were, of Christian regions and regions within us which need to be converted.

To prepare such a map is a necessity full of surprises. Do not minutes, hours, whole periods of our daily activities

pass without any awareness of the presence of God? Thus
the preponderant part of our days need to be won for him.
A church that one never enters gradually ceases to be a
real church. We must get to work and see that this temple
of God which is oneself is as truly his as it ought to be.
Away with the unknown forest and its thickets: let it be
cleared and ordered, and above all let the sunshine in. Let
there be no more sectors de-Christianized by all sorts of bad
habits, laxities, condonations, sins of the tongue, sins of the
flesh. No more unevangelized sectors of the thousand and one
needs created by the life of today, of the new problems
awaiting to be transformed by traditional spirituality and
by the presence of Christ in us.

If God were to disappear, could the Church be sure that
he would find refuge in the hearts of her people?

We must be vigilant and good missionaries in respect
to ourselves, good witnesses of Christ before ourselves.

3

THE CHURCH

UNDERSTANDING AND LOVE FOR THE CHURCH

It is our instinctive desire that we ourselves — and others through us, God willing — may know, understand, and love the Church.

In expressing this wish, we inevitably think of the weight of hostility that nearly overwhelms the Church today as ever; and we think of the massive ignorance and prejudice through which the Church must struggle.

We think also of the unwarranted freedom, which even Christians nowadays assume as a sort of point of honor, in judging the activities of the Church without restraint or appeal. Her past, her attitudes, affairs, members are all judged as unfavorably as by her worst enemies.

One sometimes thinks they do not love her. This is doubtless untrue, and their impatience often hides real generosity and desire for good. Doubtless too, many infidelities on the part of Christians are at the bottom of these condemnations of the Church. Doubtless the Church partly deserves them.

Nevertheless, in the face of complaints that are often violent, ill-considered and unfair, the Church needs faithfulness of a new sort: loyalty which is certainly not blind — for the Church loves nothing less than deceit — but consists first of all of faith which is confident, simple and loving in the sense of the love that a son has for his mother.

Filial love is a most suitable image. There are sons who bring home with them the sounds of their day's battles, the storms of strife echoing around them, recount the risks run and the new struggles that tomorrow will bring, until it hardly seems that they are still members of the family. There are others, sons and daughters, who remain at home watchful and anxious the day long, their attention on their mother, wholeheartedly attached to her by a love so tender and strong that it never occurs to them to criticize or judge her; they love, serve and obey her; they are solicitous for her, and her joys and sorrows are theirs; they spend every effort to lead the others to love her more and to find her ever more beautiful and lovable when they return home. That image is one that we find easily in our treasury of memories. The nuns of the Church are among those latter children. Their hearts are open, the love that dwells in them is no deception, and their faith is never troubled.

Their prayers throughout the year and especially in October ought to be along these lines: that understanding and love for the Church may grow. May your own love for the Church be ever keener and sparkling bright. May it contribute, by prayer and sacrifice, to the growth in other souls of true light and strength to protect them.

"Christ loved the Church and delivered himself up for her ... that he might present to himself the Church in all her glory, not having spot or wrinkle or any such thing, but that she might be holy and without blemish" (Eph. 5, 25-27).

Let each religious look within herself and find the graces that will enable her to play her own part in this common effort, rejoicing in Christ, for the glory of God in this world which is slowly regaining its faith and some charity toward the Church.

HOLY CHURCH

In the midst of present problems and the depressing atmosphere that prevails around us, it is good to think of the Church and to turn to her, to declare our love for her and to savor the pleasures of being close to her as to a mother.

The Church has the right to such homage from her children; and by this very homage, we grow better.

The pressure of laicism, which pretends to be a crusade and likes to be considered as on the defensive even where it has not been attacked, reveals the presence of a perennial enemy. It is usually masked but is now crouching in the shadows and ready to spring. Ordinarily we prefer not to believe in it.

Let us open our eyes wide, for tomorrow its tactics will be renewed, and they are the tactics of silence, of an enemy that wants to make us forget its presence.

Both the best and the worst in us allow us to spend our days peacefully ignoring the existence of hatred. The best in us, because hatred is hard to understand. The worst, because it is easier not to believe it exists. However, our Lord's words are quite blunt: *"the world hates you,"* (John 15, 19). We must know that the Church stirs up hatred — we are not to resign ourselves to it, but to know it. Hatred for the Church is, alas, one of the signs by which we recognize the presence of him whom the world first hated (cf. John 15, 18).

This thwarts our good will and troubles our spirits, but it is so. The current trials, slanders, and outrages serve to dispel our illusions. We should be wrong to try to conquer evil with anything but good (cf. Rom. 12, 21), but we should be equally wrong not to recognize the existence of evil.

The Church cannot be loved by everyone in a world that is sick (cf. I John 5, 19), for then the Church would no longer be Christ.

It is comfortable to live at peace with everyone, to choose not to believe in evil; but this creates an illusion which does no service to God because it is not based on reality.

A Christian must be strong, brave enough to battle, ready to suffer, and ever watchful (cf. I Pet. 5, 8).

The life of today helps us see it: the Church has her enemies. Yet that is probably not the worst of the situation.

Besides hatred, which is but one feature of the trouble, there is the misunderstanding and rejection on the part of those near and dear to us, neighbors, relatives, friends, people who belong to the Church and are good willed and good hearted, yet who seem at times to lose their senses.

Some laicists are crusaders, some are blind. But, often with respectable and admirable motives, they come closer and closer to working against what the Church considers her own good and proper sphere of activity. This is the worst difficulty and it is important to appreciate it.

Are we in any way responsible for the blindness? We live so closely together: what separates us? Among us Christians, something unites our hearts while dividing our spirits.

This may be partly our fault. Have people been able to see clearly and easily what we are and have wanted to be through the years? The life of a man or woman wholly given to God, dependent upon him, poor, obedient, and chaste, is strikingly conspicuous in contrast to the world we live in. And it is something that can never be contested by those of our brethren who are sincere.

If then it is possible for some Christians to belittle a way of life built on such foundations and to dispute its legitimacy, I would answer: the foundations must have been too difficult, if not impossible, to discern.

Having had a good look at hatred and incomprehension, we must do better and be more faithful. Let us have even greater charity for those who hate us or blindly oppose us.

We shall disarm hatred. We will help the blind to see. We will love more than ever.

All the hostile attitudes that we encounter are hard for one who has given herself body and soul to the service of others. She will bear it, of course, as did Jesus. Following in his steps, we cannot be astonished to find the same circumstances. Merely understand that we must do even better and more than before. And thus will we feel more deeply our membership in the Church, who struggles and grows in charity.

THE FRATERNAL UNITY OF ALL MEN IN CHRIST

This is the ultimate meaning of the mystery hidden from the beginning in the heart of God and now revealed for our rejoicing. It was the ardent desire of the heart of Jesus on the evening of the Last Supper. It is the hope that sustains the Church and inspires her zeal.

From this point of view, how does the world of today appear?

From all parts come news of wars, cold or hot, dangerous disputes, and deadlocked oppositions. Those who are un-involved in such strife are nonetheless fearful of the consequences. They foresee the possible conflicts, the resurgence of dread and disaster, the vicious circle in which hatred breeds war and war breeds hate.

It is not Christian to let oneself be carried away by such morbid prospects. Nor is it Christian to give in to fear. By faith we must rise above these storms; we must protect ourselves from their contagion, yet be willing to play our part in righting things.

We must rise above these storms by faith

Christians, we know that the unity of mankind is not entirely unaccomplished. We believe that, in a certain way, it already marvellously and really exists. We believe that the parts of the world not yet at peace nevertheless look toward that summit where the perfect communion of Saints already reigns in Christ glorified. And we know that here among us the Church already shares in this unity.

Religious have a profound share in it.

In the midst of this world that knows only how to cause or intensify divisions, it is important that *religious communities* on their part make the most of the fraternal unity which grace has created, cherish it, and make it an offering for the glory of God. One way of doing so — without doubt the most real and efficacious way — is to participate in the Church's prayers for "fraternal unity." Make this your intention every morning in each of your houses, appearing before God with sincere, candid, and courageous countenances. Let the members of each community, gathered daily for the sacrament of Christian unity, nourished with the same Bread which is Christ, carry into the world a sincere and real reflection of this unity.

We must guard ourselves against contagion

No one is quite safe from the world where passionately divisive fevers are rampant, nor from oneself where there is always some germ of sickness in the blood. We must take care that there are no enemy-occupied territories within us. Also, let us look at our frontiers and see whether we are not excluding many who belong within the circle of our friendship and prayers. There are many men and women around us worth our care and esteem, redeemed like us by Christ, to whom we never give a thought. There are some of whom we think without ever praying for them. There are those to whom we are indifferent and, because of our inclinations, consider beyond our attention. And there are some we allow ourselves, under one pretext or another, the right to dislike.

To the degree that such disinclinations exist in us, Christ is absent; and thus we ourselves, positively or negatively, contribute to the ills of the world. What shall we do then? What our Lord commanded — "Repent and believe the Gospel."

Nor is that all. *We must cooperate in righting things.* It is up to each one to see what God wants. It is up to each one to choose the object of her efforts: it may be something that moves her to generosity, or it may be something less inviting "Overcome evil with good," is St. Paul's maxim. Overcome hatred with love. Follow in the tread of him who triumphed by his cross. Pray for the unloving. Pray for those who are unloved. What joy to be called by God to this task. What gratitude do we not owe him — do you not owe him — for having manifested the joy and called us to the task?

4 *The Nun:*

THE COMMUNION OF SAINTS

The Church is a family. This figure is represented in innumerable passages in the Gospels. Jesus introduced us into a "divine society," and by that fact all of humanity shares in a mystic unity beyond the reality of words and mortal experience.

Grace has established a kinship of a unique sort between souls, a relationship that no human efforts could bring about, nor the human spirit even dream of.

Only faith in the reality of our supernatural life permits us to grasp the idea of such a brotherhood: we are brothers as truly as we are sons of God.

"As obedient children ... be you also holy in all your behavior, for it is written, You shall be holy, because I am holy. ... Now that your obedience to charity has purified your souls for a brotherly love that is sincere, love one another heartily and intensely. For you have been reborn, ... from incorruptible seed, through the word of God who lives and abides forever" (I Pet. 1, 14-15; 22-23).

Our divine sonship logically creates a brotherhood of the same nature and inspires the whole train of St. John's thought in his first epistles. One must see that in order to understand the interplay of his ideas and frequent reiterations. It is *so* obvious to him that to love God is to love one's brethren. He repeats almost passionately that love for God without brotherly love is a delusion and a lie. Likewise he insists that brotherly love without love for God is nothing. "It is all one, the one exists within the other as in the persons of the Trinity," says Pascal. *"What we have seen and have heard we announce to you, in order that you also may have fellowship with us, and that our fellowship may be with the Father and with his Son Jesus Christ"* (I John 1, 3).

* * *

In order that these truths may not remain superficial and narrowed to the field of our own experience, two remarks seem opportune. Brotherly love has roots deeper than our sentiments and it extends beyond time and space. A Christian ought fully to appreciate that.

It is this sort of gift for one another that we should pray for. It is a wonderful work for religious and for their progress.

It is of course folly to see the truth and not *do* it (cf. John 3, 21). But it is also foolish to live as if divine realities were limited only to what we can see, grasp, or experience.

That charity is a duty, we well know and assume, which is not easy, and we are constantly having to rise above manifold resistances within ourselves. But before being a duty, charity is a grace (cf. I Cor. 12). It is a gift and an inner transforming force. It is not for us to acquire it but to exploit it; not to generate it but to act upon it.

To be charitable is to begin by believing in a fraternal relationship that is infinitely more real than our good will or anything that we can desire or express.

To be charitable is to believe that the day will come when Christ will so manifest himself in us that we will give ourselves to one another as those who belong to God.

We ought always to be brotherly by conscious effort, yet we are already brothers more than we can know. There is a road to the reality of God and his love which is travelled only in the light of this revelation of a fraternal relationship of which God is the image. If only men realized that! If only a religious community where this charity is "put into practise" would keep telling itself that charity is already there by the grace of God and resides there in order to be practised!

Yet charity extends far beyond the sphere of our observation or imagination: since it is so deeply rooted, it can branch out in great breadth.

There is a marvellous attachment between the Church and all those who live in charity — a relationship as great and as harmonious as its roots. And this is why the Church is not ashamed to have recourse to the Saints: she meets them more often than she recognizes them! She finds them in God, a part of his love and reflecting this love, associated in the divine work to save us, easily accessible, near God and near us. Among these the Blessed Virgin reigns.

Some Christians have opinions that are disturbing: if one remains loyal to the Church, uses the official prayers, participates regularly in the liturgy, how can he go wrong?

Certainly to use the Saints in a superstitious way is a serious perversion. However, it is just as seriously wrong to fail to believe that the fatherhood of God is real enough to create a brotherhood that is vital, direct, and lovable. In the communion of saints there is a guarantee of a healthy spiritual balance. Let us pray that such good and simple things will be recognized by all and become part of their lives.

SENSE AND LOVE OF THE LITURGY

Religious are naturally drawn to the liturgy and pursue it with instinctive enthusiasm and spontaneous joy. However it is well for them in their enthusiasm to remember their place in the Church.

Dozens of years ago the Church was guided, obviously by Providence, to ever more perfect formulation of her official prayers; it is a need and aim that has never ceased to be supported by the faithful.

Initiative has not ceased but rather increased: — nowadays there is an abundance of books, studies, materials and organizations to produce a liturgy ever more alive and profound, intelligible, and finished. The inevitable mistakes and overemphasis have been insignificant compared to the varied and magnificent results.

What is even more striking is that the most daring movements are being made by the Church herself. Several times in this half-century the Sovereign Pontiff has led us back to original sources in order that liturgical life, like a river, might take a fresh course to renew the earth and make it to flower and bear fruit to the glory and praise of God.

When new things are good and right, one gets used to them so quickly as to forget what innovations they were. We have become too well adapted to our new privileges that we can hardly appreciate what previous generations lacked. Or that they had no notion of what they were missing.

Think of all that has resulted from the bold spirit of St. Pius X. Think of all the innovations of these past few years. Who would think of comparing our grandparents' missals to those you and I use?

However, we well know that this new grace which is refreshing the Church awaits our cooperation to produce its fruit.

A religious ought to be more alert than anyone to the

value of this grace: she ought to understand it, rejoice in
it, be the first to abandon herself to it and seek the develop-
ment of its truths. By her vocation and state of life, given
and consecrated to God, ought she not to be consequently
keenly sensitive to the things of God and his glory and honor?

By her profession she has entered upon a way of life of
God's own ordering. More than a church, an altar of stone,
or a golden chalice, which are but *things*, she belongs to
him as a creature of mind and soul devoted to his glory.
What she withholds or allows to be withdrawn from him
is bound to be sacrilege.

So then, she takes a natural part in the liturgy: she is
at home. She rejoices to see and hear God glorified. She
contributes voice and heart and her whole self. She was
predestined to participate in and to pass on this new spirit
in the Church. Only disloyalty would cause her to refuse it.

She may however refuse by pouting and not going along
with "these innovations." But if the novelties are officially
authorized, then she is in fact pouting at the Church! Let
her then enter into a world reawakening with the sunlight
of new grace: let her pray more than ever the prayers of
the Church, particularly the psalms; let her not only participate in the liturgy but also encourage those in her charge
to do so.

She will bring to it her own offering — something which
no one else can offer to the same degree — the sense that
liturgy is above all *divine*.

Humans and earthlings that we are, even the Mass can
lose some of its original intentions; it may tend to become
a merely human effort and communal demonstration rather
than a divine gift and sacrifice to God. "Unto the praise of

the glory of his grace," is St. Paul's refrain in his epistle to
the Ephesians, and it is the aim of all liturgy — and of all
that we do.

The nun bears witness to this aim because the liturgy
demands it, because she takes part in it gladly, appreciates
more than anyone its richness, and because she wants its
benefits to be shared. By her prayers, may it be revealed
to all who do not yet know it that the praise of God is
man's chief joy.

4

THE CONVENT

REGULATIONS

Regulations mean mortification.

We accept this with good hearts since we know that we are far from him whom we receive in our daily communions and whom we cannot expect to reach except by following in the way of the Cross. But are we equally ready to accept mortification wherever God appoints it, especially in humdrum perseverance rather than in efforts that are heroic but transient?

It seems worthwhile to challenge, as it were, the idea of mortification with that of regularity. The very fact that the word "regularity" is uninspiring — or even distasteful to some — in itself shows where true mortification is to be sought.

Our Lord received from his Father an *agenda*. He accomplished it. In every detail. Nor did he die until he had accomplished all the prophecies of the Redemption. *"That the scripture might be fulfilled,"* our Lord evaded nothing. At every point from Bethlehem to the Cross he represented his Father.

"There is a time to be born and a time to die" (Eccles. 3, 2), and our Lord awaited his hour. It all could have been accomplished in an instant, by a *fiat*. Yet there were the thirty silent years — useless? empty? — recorded in the Gospel in only a few words. What was there to record?

His life was not unknown yet people thought it uneventful.

Likewise a direct act could have enlightened the apostles, and our Lord could have spared himself the longsuffering days when the least of his words was misunderstood by their poor minds and faint hearts. The enthusiasm of the day of Pentecost could have been created immediately. Yet that was not the Father's plan, and his Son never swerved from it.

There is a vast difference between our Lord's idea of perfection and our own; between the divine agenda and our accomplishments. This is partly because we are so little inclined to see regularity, with the self-denial it entails, as a way of perfection. We hardly consider it a real expression of the will of God.

Rather than delude ourselves, it is better to confess the humiliating facts that our wills and the divine will often clash, and that our love is not strong enough.

Our love for the rule can be measured only by our love for God; indeed it is not the rule itself which is to be loved but only the divine will of which it is a sign and guide. So let us not keep blinding ourselves to the fact that regularity is the great means of remaining faithful to his will.

The present world does not share this view. Impulsiveness, individualism, and private whims are virtues sacred to our time and we have almost gotten to the point of believing that without them we are lacking in devotion. Even whole religious communities can be threatened by this contemporary contagion. So it is imperative for us to fall back upon the Gospel and try to exorcise the demons that beguile our natural little desires.

To arise early in silence and without delay: is this a

great mortification? Has a religious any more excuse for indulging in whims or laziness than a simple mother of a family whose children await her? The mortification of being punctual at daily offices and appointments is of divine will. How many inconveniences, annoyances, and disagreements — not to mention further troubles — are caused in a community by tardiness so habitual as to be almost neurotic.

Then there is the mortification of fulfilling personal duties at the regular times. We know from experience that to postpone a confession, a rosary, a chapter of spiritual reading, or whatever, generally means to omit it altogether.

These are small things, you say. No, therein lies the real mortification. *There* is the regularity that wipes out the nameless and innumerable little desires that appear innocent but are a malign influence, desires which can slowly grow into a complete and permanent complex in an imperceptibly paralyzing network.

Everything at God's hour and not at our own. Everything at the appointed time. What mortification and what an aid to perfection! What a blessing to others. But above all, what a joy to offer to God.

"I am never alone. The Father is always with me . . . because I do always his will." Who can stop us from appropriating Jesus' words to ourselves? In them are truth and joy.

SPIRITUAL EXERCISES

The title that St. Ignatius chose for his precious "Directory" has become famous. It is in common usage and currently denotes the regular activities of the religious life carried out privately or in common — meditation, examen, office, etc. Faithfulness in these "exercises" serves as an honest measure of our real faithfulness and also guards against lukewarmness on the one hand or fancifulness on the other.

It would be rash and presumptuous to try to live the religious life without these exercises: their regular, uniform, fixed and somewhat ascetic character is bound to keep the soul in the hand of God. They keep us from rushing too fast spiritually, at the risk of going off the track; they keep us from following a sudden inspiration, it is true, but only to guard us from delusion. They may deprive one of some spiritual comforts or rewards, yet they keep alive the invaluable sense of the necessity of painstaking effort and are the salt that, even though it stings, prevents infection.

All prudent self-examination must center around these exercises, and it is a mistake to take them lightly. To take account of them, being strict with ourselves although never overscrupulous, is the way of assurance. For the Church understands them to be God's will and wishes us to do so.

The word "exercise" means something slightly painful, requiring a certain effort, and which is not an end in itself. One exercises in order to overcome weaknesses, to strengthen oneself and in fact to enable oneself to achieve some goal or end that is already in sight and desirable.

One "meditates" in order to penetrate divine truth and to let it penetrate, i.e., to open oneself to the action of grace and to clear the way for the light and love of the Holy Spirit, that we may see and do better. Meditation is not an end in itself: one does not throw logs on a fire or stir up the embers just for the sake of exercise, but to kindle flames. The fire demands the effort, but the effort is made for the sake of the warmth.

Likewise, one does not make a particular or general examen for the sake of self-appraisal. When this is the case, as it sometimes is, it is wrong. One makes a self-examination out of love for God, to expose oneself to his light, and to see better what pleases or displeases him. When we stop short of such an end to an examen, we become befogged; a haziness overclouds our judgment, we are confused, and our vices take deeper root. An examen prompted by anxiety or accompanied by complacency is useless. Our self-examinations must be to determine whether we are on the right path, whether we are pleasing to the God whom we love, and worthy of him.

Moreover, you are bound to a rule that regulates hours, apportions time, and fixes the appointments of life. Greater liberty often seems desirable: one can pray better at another hour or in different circumstances. But it could be that you would not pray at all were it not for the rule! A stimulus of today inviting you to seek some unappointed time or place for prayer may have evaporated by tomorrow. The rule conserves both today's and tomorrow's efforts.

A nun ought to appreciate her unusual privileges in the world in which we live; she ought thankfully to compare her very favorable situation with the common lot of those plodding daily through an existence that seems purposeless, with its perpetual striving that comes to nothing.

Yes our "exercises" are a bondage. The bondage is not merely a superficial one. It is a real limit to the scope of initiative and choice, and it eliminates what is called luck. It saves us from numerous, often material, choices for the sake of things that are primary: interior and more important choices for the sake of the greatest and only true choice, which is the divine will, and in and through it the love of God.

A rule insures one against the worst danger nowadays: the failure to give oneself, and to surrender in the unending and ever-shifting battle of life. Meanwhile the enormous energy necessary for this must be drawn from a retreat or day of recollection. Otherwise, heroic attempts fall into irreparable ruins.

The truth is that regular spiritual exercises are a marvellous luxury. One feels sorry for those who do not grasp what God offers through them and who are misled by dreams of some broader or more liberal way. Actually it is the regular exercises which keep under control the faults in us which really endanger true liberty and true love. "An hour of truth" when we look at ourselves with complete honesty is the hour when the Master will come. Then there will be no more time for delay or self-deception: the one question will be, What do we want him to do with our lives?

Happy will be the man or woman able to trace a line of regularity where the "exercises" have kept one turned to God, moving toward him step by step, quietly, diligently, and without haste. Grand deeds will seem but a small thing beside a regularity that is uniform and stern. The road, hard and bleak though it may be, will seem to us full of grace and benediction despite the meadows and flowers we have had to by-pass.

"I am the way," said our Lord. It is no overstatement to say that his is the way of the "exercises." If we fix that in our minds, we will come to love it despite the burden that is but one of the many forms that compose the cross. Therein is truth.

CHRISTIAN FRIENDSHIP

*"You are my friends. . . . No longer do I call you servants.
but friends . . ."* (John 15, 14-15).

Friendship. The Gospel is so shot through with such
simple words of inexhaustible meaning that we cease to
hear them or else believe that we have long ago fully explored
their meaning.

They are like the wildflowers of which St. Thérèse speaks
in the beginning of *The History of a Soul* — violets and
Easter daisies that we accidentally and carelessly trample
under foot, unmindful that they form the very setting that
we find refreshing.

The friendship of Jesus Christ! The brotherly love that
is born of Christ: *"Love one another . . . as I have loved
you"* (John 13, 34). The word "friendship" is one which
has best resisted the wretched abasement of so many words
in our language. Think of what the world has done to the
word "love."

Fortunately one can still find in the word friendship
something of the purity and charity associated with the
presence of God and which lifts us out of ourselves.

I realized that recently, when I had the joy of meeting
several hundred nuns gathered for a period of study of
hospital and social work, I thought of it in terms of "friendship," a word which I had much on my mind, and which
pointed not only to great resources of grace but also to
the great hopes that it could inspire. I told myself that it
could be and indeed is a joy to God the creator, the same
joy recorded in Genesis where he surveys all that he has
created and calls it good — or the joy of a Father whose
kingdom has come.

So our poor world is not simply one of division, hostility or hatred. We must realize this personally and rejoice with God, in order to experience our wonderful communion with the heart of God despite all the darknesses.

It takes some trouble to create friendship; for here on earth charity is a "commandment," and we experience it as such day after day when there is so much rebellion within and around us. Yet friendship is also the source of our healthiest and happiest joys and of the pleasures that are simplest and most disinterested.

Friendship within a community, even to outsiders, is always the most striking and appealing fulfillment of our Lord's words, *"By this will all men know that you are my disciples, if you have love for one another"* (John 13, 35).

One would like friendship to come easily, to be comforting, rewarding, and not cost much. And this is liable to cause relationships to degenerate into pseudo-friendships or, as we say, "special friendships," which are in fact a contradiction of divine love, a plague on the community, the worm in the apple.

Friendship is *universal*, as in Christ. It is *crucified*, as Christ. It is *disinterested*, as he was. It is not of this world: it depends on promises of a kingdom to come. Do not be beguiled into thinking that it can be otherwise.

It is enough to unmask the danger to know how to avert it. Real friendship of the sort that contains sparks of eternal joy can only be an enlargement and extension, in human relations, of friendship with Christ. Its characteristics grew out of its real source. Far from hindering devotion, it evokes and demands and nourishes it. It cannot be exclusive, for Christ is party to it, and it must be orientated to his love for all mankind.

Choices and preferences there may rightly be. John was known as the disciple whom Jesus loved. Yet Peter was loved too, and what greater witness is there than the passionate conversation, *"Simon, dost thou love me? . . ."*

It is certainly right to prefer to love the family into which God has called one to live the religious life; but such love, if it is born of God, can be denied to no one.

May God show all the sisters who enjoy such love that it is not only the greatest sign of his presence among them but also the deepest assurance that their prayers will be heard, as he promised.

Give, O Lord, to all these souls this understanding of friendship and the desire to keep it, with confidence that they are pleasing you and that their efforts are not in vain.

THE SICK

It will be a good thing for nuns to reconsider their service to the sick. For some, it will be a matter of reappraising the profound grace that has dedicated them to this ministry; others ought to see and notice what an urgently important form of charity it is, with providential demands not to be pushed aside.

Let us salute for once those in our various communities whose vocation is to care for the sick. The sick are so tiresome, and our encounters and responsibilities seem such a nuisance when we have important things to do! We do not let the patients we visit tie us down or encroach on our freedom: we know that at the end of the visit we will be free again; so it is relatively easy to be gracious and solicitous, spend a few minutes, say some kind words. Soon we will be rid of the chore; we do not use the word "rid" or even think it, but alas, who will deny that it is often in our hearts?

Basically it amounts to this: in agreeing to give something, we must end by giving ourselves. *"He who loses his life for my sake will find it"* (Matt. 10, 39). The sick in the neighborhood or in the house, or the sister too ill to work, all demand care and attention — and what they really and specifically need is ourselves. We must be with them when they want us.

I do not hesitate to say that the spiritual quality of any community is to be judged by the manner in which the elderly, the sick, and the invalids are treated. The judgment will depend on how sure they are of the joy of being loved and of not being alone.

In any case, can any community brush aside this endowment? For it is a capital endowment, an investment in the suffering that belongs to the kingdom of God. One of the greatest benefits to be looked for among Christians is the discovery of the sick as a redemptive force with apostolic power.

Nuns ought to pray that this be realized. But they cannot so pray without appreciating the immediate needs of their own sisters.

The task is not to speak encouraging words to a sister who is ill; it is rather to *believe* that she has more power for good than we have. It is also to help her herself to believe it; to help her to see that, despite pain and discouragement, she is the object of God's attention and also an instrument of his saving grace.

When God calls us someday to the same situation, perhaps we will be better prepared for it, having seen it in others.

May all the sick, aged, and suffering in our communities feel themselves sustained by the faith and love of those around them.

OUR DEAD

We must realize that the departed are more and more forgotten by the hearts and minds of the people of today. There is a new indifference no longer to be excused merely as forgetfulness. It has deep causes touching on the faith itself. Insofar as one sees signs of it in oneself, one must beware of the same causes and dangers.

Are the sisters who compose our religious communities in any way guilty? What place in their thoughts has death or remembrance of the departed? To question oneself on these points has become a duty.

Why do we think so little of death? Partly because it is so familiar and commonplace. Who can count all those who have died in the wars of yesterday and today on battlefield far and near? People are killed on the highways and the toll of each holiday weekend is predicted in advance. By public demand the newspapers feature each day's accidents, crimes, or suicides. Death has become a stupid happening.

On the other hand, we cling to life in this threatening universe as something more precious than ever, indeed the only precious thing. We shield it from others and from accidents. We have no time to look beyond the present moment. Living as feverishly preoccupied and anxious as we are, the all important thing seems to be the fragile space of time in which we are allowed to live and, if possible, be happy. As a result, death ceases to be an event for which we stop to prepare ourselves. The dead disappear into the night and even the faithful hesitate to gaze after them.

Never has it been more important to hearken to the word of God which alone can lift us out of the torpor. His words invite us to think of the moment of death as more important than life itself; they tell us that Christ's resurrection and ours are not empty promises.

This means, not that we are to disdain life, but rather that we be more sensitive to the gravity of each hour — one of which will be the hour of death and decide our eternal destiny. *"Watch and pray, for it comes like a thief in the night."*

There is no better aid to this train of thought than devout and deliberate remembrance of our beloved dead. To act as if they were no more than objects of vague regret or sorrowing sentiments is to do them an injustice. To many of them we owe much. We lack charity, when our prayers can help them. And we betray the truth, for any minimization of the importance of the resurrection is an open road to heresy.

Every community should examine itself and its customs in this respect. Common prayers and the offering of Mass keep love alive. They also strengthen us and those for whom we are responsible.

CHILDREN

Nuns naturally think readily and warmly of children. The divine regard for them is remarkable: the Gospel shows our Lord's tenderness to children, his adamance about their protection and his desire that we care about their welfare with a divine jealousy that never slackens.

So many religious institutions have been born of this divine love for children; and they have been the vocation of many saintly foundresses.

Kindness, affection, attachment. God asks more than naturally spontaneous sentiment.

He is no respecter of persons: the less graceful child or the disgraceful one is also his own. He does not tire: the difficult child is his too. He is not self-seeking: to love is to give. He does not give up: in the end he let himself be nailed to his cross. That is the sort of love that God charges us to give to his little ones, to the least of his little ones. This love cannot but come from the heart, and the child needs our hearts. Sometimes it happens that our hearts are cold: then charity must take over.

The love that God asks us to give to his children must be as strong as it is tender, as patient, as joyful, as demanding as it is indulgent. For it is *his* love.

Women whom God has called to this work and endowed with sure resources of his love ought to have great confidence, pride, and joy. They must work hard to be faithful to the task and we must pray for them. Pray that their love may be pure and the divine love shine brightly through them; that they may not hinder his grace nor hold back anything that is his; their honor and riches are in serving. Pray that their love may be strong and patient and that no sentimental softness may ever be an obstacle to the beneficial firmness of the divine love, which molds a child into a man and a son of God. Pray that their love lead them to accept God's overwhelming preference for the littlest, the humblest, the poorest, the one who is lost.

When a child is so stubborn, mean, or unlovable as to exhaust our efforts and hopes, God replies, "The child is mine." Therefore it must be *ours*. No one loves it? Yes, God does and we do.

Pray for those nuns whom God has chosen, endowed, and taught to understand that dialogue and to act accordingly.

Pray for the families. The child's life is centered in the family, and his whole being inclines to the father and mother of whose flesh God has made him.

Pray that our teachers remain sincerely and deeply respectful of this principle, and use all their resources and generosity to serve the "child as a member of a family," not apart from or in spite of the family, which would be detrimental to the child and to the divine will.

Difficult? All that matters is that it can be done. It can because God asks it. How? When we want to, we will find a way.

Pray that God will give those in charge of the children enough love for the undertaking, and imagination and perseverance.

When nuns pray for the children, they pray both *as* religious and *for* the religious, so their prayers cannot be in vain.

5

THE CALENDAR

CHRISTMAS AND THE NEW YEAR

For the Church, Christmas and the ending of the year are blended, and thus we are entirely turned toward the future. For Christmas Day is a birthday. And what a birth! that of Jesus, God-with-us.

The liturgy, which is a sure guide and natural expression of the Church's life, seems to ignore our common sentiment as an old year gives place to a new. In many Christian countries it is on Christmas Day that one says, Happy New Year; for the symbolic and legal importance that we attach to December 31st and January 1st is not universal.

The Church forgets nothing but does not look back. She does not condemn an observance of New Year's Eve with a Holy Hour or litany and self-examination, but she wishes such things to draw their inspiration from the liturgy.

There is but one good way of life on the circling globe and the human heart well knows it: it is to live in the spirit of Christmas.

The events of our own lives, whether serious or trivial, ought not to govern our participation in the holy mysteries of the faith. It should be the other way round: the divine mysteries should order and dominate our own manner of facing the thousand incidents and accidents of personal and social life.

The holy events of our Lord's life neither minimize nor overshadow the realities of simple human existence. We know well that our God can weep with us: his name is Jesus, he loved Lazarus, he accepted the Cross. We are well aware of how he prized our happiness and died for it. "Rejoice and exult," he said in his Sermon on the Mount.

He is not indifferent to our little joys and sorrows: how could he be when he is our *friend*? Our remembrances of mundane events important only to us form a part of our lives, and it would belittle our Lord's friendship to suppose that he did not care.

Yet how far superior he is to all these things that evoke our sentiments, whether sweet or dramatic, and so easily distort our sense of proportion and reduce great mysteries to the level of passing emotions.

Jesus is far from being a master without a heart. Yet he is equally far from being as sweet as he is often pictured. Both images are wrong. He knows every one of our tears; yet the purpose of his sympathy is to begin to restore. He loves us too forcefully to let us be buried in sentiment while our wills dissolve.

New Year's Eve brings the great totalling up of the bill, an enormous sum. There is an incalculable conglomeration of all sorts of events, exterior and interior, from which emerge a smattering of facts, good deeds, and misspent emotions. Next year at the same time there will be the same bill and one will hardly see any difference.

Why put it off? Why delay in recognizing that one condition is permanent? Namely, that when our Lord has a part in them, the contact of divine charity eternalizes all things — all joys, all sorrows, including fears, however human.

Once more it is time to bring to him what has not already been kindled by his flame. It is time to throw another year,

such as it was, on his fire; the fire of our God who has just
been born, in whom all find themselves, apart from whom
all are lost.

If for us the end of the year is Christmastide and the
Nativity of our Lord occupies our minds as it does the
Church, then the bill will be easy to total and we will be
glad to pay it.

What good have we accomplished? any of us or any of
our communities? What ought we try to do in the coming
year? These questions must be deep in our hearts. The
Church is content to answer: it is Christmas. You know
him: he is the one to listen to your hearts and answer your
questions.

No one who is wise will consider the Church indifferent
to our feelings because of her apparent silence in respect to
New Year's Day. The old year has been spent, but there
is the Nativity. The new year is full of uncertainties, but
there is the Nativity.

Holy Church speaks to us in this fashion, and this is
the word of God: *"When the goodness and kindness of
God our Savior appeared, then not by reason of good works
that we did ourselves, but according to his mercy, he saved
us . . . in order that, justified by his grace, we may be heirs
in the hope of life everlasting"* (Titus 3, 4-7).

PENITENCE, PENITENCE

A hundred and some years ago now, on a bleak winter
morning in a rocky setting on the bank of the Gave, the
Blessed Virgin appeared to a young woman. There was a

conversation which forever engaged Bernadette and engages all who are drawn to Lourdes.

The Church does not hesitate to keep her people aware of these facts, for the strengthening of their faith, and in order that they may discover in happenings close to us the reality of eternal things, which are even closer but seem to vanish from sight when we touch them.

It is a good thing to make a pilgrimage to Lourdes, at least in spirit. The Blessed Virgin has all sorts of things to say to us. Rather, she waits to tell us things we already know, the only saving things, in a way that will lead us to accept and love them better. How much Lourdes resembles the Gospel, for anyone willing to open her heart and listen.

How the life of a religious resembles Lourdes for any nun who expects no more of God than what he wishes to say and repeat.

How wonderfully Lourdes proclaims the Gospel. One cannot but be tempted to compare the simple and clear words of the apparitions with the simplicity and clarity of the beginning of St. Luke's Gospel — the announcement to Mary, and to the world, of the incarnation.

One cannot go wrong here, for the words are all of the same source and inspiration, of the same Spirit. The one guarantees the other. It is the same heart and soul, the same Mary, who listens to the angel and who speaks to Bernadette. It is the same Spirit who gives Mary grace to understand the angel's message and who moves her to speak to Bernadette according to God's will.

The faithful and simple response of Bernadette is the replica of Mary's. An innocent girl, ignorant of evil and wishing to know none, unpretentious and simply putting

herself at God's disposal, strong in humility and, because
of her humility, strong and firm in reacting to the divine
word: such was Mary and so was Bernadette to be.

With the passage of time and the revelation of things
in their true light, we see Mary in the incomparable grandeur
of her motherhood and see Bernadette in the light of her
heroic sanctity. However the Gospel reminds us rather bluntly
of the true source and nature of their greatness when an
unknown Jewess in a crowd exclaims, *"Blessed is the womb
that bore thee."* We call Bernadette saintly and Mary glorious,
rightly so as long as we recall the real reasons; and that is
why our Lord stopped and said, *"Rather, blessed are they
who hear the word of God and keep it"* (Luke 11, 27-28).

It was not by chance that Bernadette became a nun
and that she sought the obscurity of the Nevers convent
in which to bury her secret, meditate upon it, and cherish
its inner meanings. The chastity, poverty, and obedience
that she vowed and lived so far from Lourdes were not at
all in contrast to her call; indeed her vocation was *realized*
in humility and penitence.

A nun who finds some disappointment in a contrast
between the extraordinary heavenly favor granted to Bernadette and her consequent enclosure at Nevers betrays that
she understands neither Bernadette's holiness nor the meaning of the religious life itself.

The Gospel does not change. The Beatitudes are for the
meek, the poor, the singlehearted. This is what charity and
holiness come to.

One can make a fine Lent hand in hand with Bernadette:
by saying humbly with her the rosary which the Blessed
Virgin taught her, by tasting with her the bittersweet savor of

penitence, silence, and obedience, by giving up, along with her, all that is contrary to the divine will, by relearning from her wherein the true Christian strength lies — surely only in God.

Saint Bernadette, help us not to be mistaken nor to let worldly greatness usurp in our desires and judgments the true supernatural greatness of the Gospel and of our crucified Lord.

THE CHURCH PREPARES FOR EASTER

One must always beware lest the great mysteries of the faith focus too narrowly upon oneself. Or to put it another way, *I* and what *I* need distort my perspective of divine events and promises, and an insistence of *my* relationship with God often effectively blocks the flow of grace, and certainly impedes it. Unless it is real egoism, it is an optical illusion rather than a moral failure.

A religious, having a special vocation and chosen by the divine will, is especially susceptible to this danger; to be recollected and detached can end in being isolated.

In that case it becomes difficult for her to say even *"Our* Father . . ." ! All our prayers must be inadequate unless they accord with that prayer.

How may a nun discover the right point of distinction between care for personal salvation — so emphasized by our Lord in his warning to *"watch and pray"* — and the nurture of her religious vocation — also so personal, since she is a "spouse, uniquely beloved"— and the common good? The common good is the salvation of all mankind. Is the answer, *"She who finds her life will lose it"*?

Who can judge where the right point lies? There is one who is in a good position to do so, and indeed it is her mission: it is the Church.

If we are willing and able to listen to the Church, to sit at her feet and follow her thoughts, we will not have to wrack our brains to find the answer. Lingering and praying with her, we shall not *find* the right point, for we shall *be* there.

The Church lives intensely in Lent and Paschaltide; all her being is in action as in a great undertaking with tremendous stakes. It is the Church's springtime.

All her forces are at work like the hidden powers that make a tree burst into bloom. There is long deadness to be revived and new branches to be produced. The sap is rising through veins old and new, and it will irresistibly renew the foliage and revitalize the tree.

At Easter everything ought to be new, that the young Christ may exult in his new-born faithful, that the Father may be glorified in his Son, and the Son in a Church without spot or wrinkle. It is an explosive operation extending to every part of the tree, to each cell where death has done its work and where life will accomplish its own.

That is why the Church demands so much. Each day's liturgy changes; it is more highly organized than an army, and as systematic; it is lengthy and ever more elegant. Like the sap nourished by all sorts of roots, the liturgy stems from the rich soil of Holy Scripture fertile with the words of the ancient prophets and with those of our Lord. They reverberate from infinity: penitence, justice, love.

Make ready the Lord's Passover and ours. Do not fail to be present at the cross or at the resurrection. It is the day of the Church's renewal.

5 *The Nun:*

As for ourselves, will we share this spirit or be mere spectators? Will we watch this renewal and remain apart from it? My private Lent, indeed! My Lent is my part of the Church's Lent. It is my joyous and whole-hearted participation in a truimphant springtime. It means the pruning of the dead wood of the tree which is myself. And it means my right to have a real part in the rejoicing of Easter morning, and in the flowering of Christ, which is his before it is mine.

Yes, the penitence and sacrifice will be mine. It takes a heart to offer them, an individual human heart, and that is what is asked of me. And certainly the joy will be mine, for it is offered to me and where can it exist but in a human heart?

Yet the more we enter into the life of the Church, the more we appreciate that nothing is solitary or narrowly individual; and the more we understand that to lose all is to find everything.

The call that Christ addresses to a nun is personal only because he asks such complete abandonment. In the end we will realize that this abandonment's name is Love. There is a way of loving that is reserved: it is not the best.

How do we rightly balance personal interest and the common good? What are the right proportions of care for the Church and nurture of our own souls? Only the Church knows. She reveals it to those who accept her ways.

In Lent the Church is mightily strengthened by those who keep the Church's Lent. "True joy is to give." The greatest joy is self-giving — and we refer to Jesus himself. Then we find ourselves, or rather, God finds us. And this is just what we wanted, isn't it?

FAITH IN THE RESURRECTION

"O death, where is thy victory?" (I Cor. 15, 55).

Christians believe in the resurrection of the body: first and above all in Christ's resurrection, then in ours in him and with him. This belief puts great demands on our faith, but it fundamentally transforms those who truly accept it. There are not a few Christians who live *"kept in servitude by the fear of death"* (Hebr. 2, 15), to all appearances *"even as others who have no hope"* (I Thess. 4, 13). By our confident faith, we must strengthen the hopes of others.

In the soul vowed to God, the thought of death and its approach can but arouse great joy. *"... desiring to depart and to be with Christ, a lot by far the better"* (Phil. 1, 23). *"Him, though you have not seen, you love. In him, though you do not see him, yet believing, ye exult with a joy unspeakable..."* (I Pet. 1, 8).

What elation we find in St Thérèse of Lisieux in the terrible hours of her dying, when her faith never ceased to support her and she cried, "I will believe ... My God, I love you."

A religious who belongs to Christ alone will not confuse sentiment with fidelity in that realm. Consolations are to be welcomed but not expected or sought after. Our chief companion will be a lively faith and thoughts of the resurrection and promises more real than appearances suggest. Faith in the resurrection is an act of honesty and right understanding and it ought also to be an act of brotherly love.

First, an act of *honesty*, for the religious has pledged her faith. The union between her and Christ is no less firmly sealed than the mutual consent in a human marriage.

The human union brings immediate joys as mutual faith and love animate and purify it and make it, in faithful love and chaste fertility, a means of eternal happiness.

Union with Christ by religious profession is entirely a matter of faith. It implies the sacrifice of immediate happiness; the love that the spouse bears within her does not seek satisfaction in this world; there is no bargain made, for the word is meaningless in the realm of love. Yet it would be shamefully absurd if a bride of Christ, adorned with his promises, did not await with emotion the moment of first encounter, face to face, unveiled. ". . . *the eyes of your mind being enlightened, so that you may know what is the hope of his calling*" (Eph. 1, 18).

A religious is unfaithful if she does not live in hope for that moment. Indeed, how can she live without it?

In fact, it is a question of pure common sense.

With a sort of fury, St. Paul emphasizes the absurdity of a Christian existence unless the resurrection is true —"*Vain then is our preaching, vain too is your faith. . . . If with this life only in view we have had hope in Christ, we are of all men the most to be pitied*" (I Cor. 15, 14-19).

It is toward the meeting with Christ that everything is directed. This is what calls for present sacrifices, preparation, and detachment. If that be true for all Christians, how much more so for a nun? What sense has the religious life if the resurrection has not its proper place and its hour awaited?

A walk in the dark with Calvary and sad resignation at the end?

That is not what Christ thinks as he beckons to his own.

His choices and promises are not frauds, but we can make them so.

It is not only that we harm ourselves. If we hope, the world can learn hope through us.

To be caught in the quicksand of today's affairs or enshrouded in present actualities has always been a perennial danger to men's happiness.

They must see that there is more to life than this. We must be to them the rays of an eternal dawn shining across the night: *"a lamp shining in a dark place, until the day dawns and the morning star rises in your hearts"* (II Pet. 1, 19).

The world needs the hope of Christians; it needs the example of lives entirely dependant upon the Other Life, drawn and helped there by Christ, buoyed up by the voice that called across the water to St. Peter, "Come."

Even more than fervent prayer for those without hope, God needs the lively hopefulness of his own flock. Once more, what this means for religious is that they be themselves. Nothing else, nothing more, is asked of the nun. Nothing is greater or more precious.

PASCHAL JOY

Our paschal joy is a very delicate treasure. How can we guard and keep it from the slow dissipation that usually happens to all our interior goods? Like those artificial satellites that men are launching into space, which disintegrate as soon as they return to the atmosphere of the earth, so our paschal joys seem to quickly spent and dissolved by the pressures of daily life.

Yet was it a precarious gift? That is not God's usual

way: he does not withdraw himself from his gifts. Rather, he has willed, *"that your joy may be full and that it may remain."*

Yes, paschal joy can last, for it is nothing but God's own joy. It must endure in those who really possess it and let it be seen so that the world may know where true joys lie.

Now what are the conditions for preserving this joy? First, that we make a clear distinction between what in our hearts is paschal joy and what is not. Next, that we well recognize its source and not look for it where it cannot be found. Finally, that we remind ourselves that this gift cannot be kept selfishly when by its very nature it is something to be shared.

Such are the conditions in which paschal joy may thrive, and no one in the world will be able to take it away from us. Everything will make it grow. Nothing could be more certain.

Paschal joy does not exclude other happiness, but it is not to be confused with any other. It is the same joy that filled the heart of the risen Christ and is now poured out upon us.

This is Jesus, who died once and lives for evermore. This is the Lamb, who was slain, of St. John's Apocalypse, *"and they fell down and worshipped him who lives forever and ever."* It is the risen Christ whom we receive in Holy Communion and paschal joy finds its real meaning in this. It is the joy of being united with Jesus risen from the dead.

Alas, this joy is sometimes spurned, and one does not have to be a great sinner or a poor Christian to do so. One can prefer other things and refuse this. It is possible not to love Jesus enough (although he is the cause of all our joy) to be happy simply because he is happy.

Quietly and secretly, I can dream of another joy: it

will be mine and I will be the principal feature. And while
I plumb the depths of this joy, the real one vanishes!

The joy which is Jesus' own and which he shares with
us does not come cheaply. We keep it only on consideration
of sharing it and by giving ourselves to the accomplishment
of its redemptive work on earth.

Paschal joy belongs only to those who are willing to
suffer, contradictory though it may seem. Think of St.
Thérèse of Lisieux whom God sought out in the midst of
Easter Day's dinner to suggest that "she sit at a table of
sinners and share their filthy bread." She lost there none of
her Easter joy; rather, she won it all, forever, during the
dramatic last years of her life. Each of us has a similar
opportunity.

That is why our Lord at the Last Supper, warning his
friends of his departure, told them with such emotion of
the coming of the Spirit, to whom he gave the mysterious
name of "Paraclete," "Defender," to convey an idea of
someone beside them and in them. *"I shall not leave you
as orphans."*

Someone watches over our paschal joy and his name is
twofold: love and sacrifice. He is no other than the Holy
Spirit, mystical ambassador of the Father and the Son. It is
he who constantly brings Jesus to us. No passionate efforts
on our part can bring us or keep this divine joy, for it belongs
to him. But he offers it, makes us new and alive, and creates
a stronghold against all that opposes it.

What an extraordinary promise! Yet it is true. At any
moment, on every occasion that we need to find him, he is
there: in our hearts where we alone recognize him. There
do we feel the mysterious touch of the Holy Spirit recalling
the divine will and empowering us to love it.

This brings us the sudden joy of victory, the paschal joy, Jesus' joy of triumph over evil, the one true, unchangeable joy; for it is the joy of doing the Father's will. And that is our daily bread. Impossible? Who dares say so?

Is it necessary to repeat that paschal joys cannot be ours unless we are ready to share them? We know where the divine will leads: we have only to reread our Credo and look in the direction of the kingdom of eternal life. We know Jesus' wish: that all mankind be saved and come to a knowledge of the truth. The Spirit who dwells in us and is the cause of our joy is the Spirit of love, and it is he who sanctifies the Church.

In the end, everything is harmoniously tied together. The present sadness and the joy that is stronger ... sorrow and hope ... it is the Spirit who teaches us that and makes us understand and accept it. The eve of Pentecost brings both the affirmation of Easter joy and the impetus for great apostolic deeds.

THE PASCHAL MYSTERY

Beyond our Lent, Paschaltide shines on the horizon. We await the blessed day. We come to it by degrees, as one climbs a mountain: each step is an effort and every step more tiring than the last; we notice nothing but the ground and can hardly think of anything but our fatigue. Then suddenly there is the summit! the glorious view of the landscape lies before our eyes in all its beauty and we stand dazed and enraptured as we see where we have climbed.

As it is with the mountain climber, so it was with the

apostles and devoted women as they wended their ways to the sepulchre in the hours before dawn: suddenly they came upon the luminous angels and the astounding fact of the resurrection, and those who first met the risen Lord were overwhelmed. So it may be with us, if we will. And of course we would and do wish it so.

However, it means to wish to be one of the women who came to the sepulchre at dawn and found the holy angels, or even to identify with her whom our Lord called so gently by name, Mary, who had "loved much."

What then should one wish? In contrast to the holy women on whom the light of the resurrection had not yet dawned, we now know the glorious end of the story. Their hearts were heavy; they loved him; that was all. He had been put to death; since they could no longer hear or see him alive, they would care for his body; they could not neglect him. They did not think further than that, except to wonder, who moved the stone? They loved him: that was all. But we know!

The resurrection is a fact and we know that we are not to *"seek the living among the dead"* (Luke 24, 5). We know that Christ arose, showed himself to his disciples, poured out his Spirit upon them, and for two thousand years has been at work on earth and in the midst of us.

It is a matter of faith. *Therefore* it is a stronger thing than passive agreement to something beyond comprehension to which we give bewildered consent; for faith comes from God and is his gift (Eph. 2, 8). It demands that we freely open our hearts and minds to the word of God. So it is not only a question of *knowing*: we must believe, and the truest paschal joy comes at that price. So we must try to find in our hearts, even though the resurrection is real to us, something of the warm attachment of those holy women drawn to the sepulchre only by the light of his blessed passion, bearing their own little lamps of love that it enkindled.

In other words, it means to have the same affection for our *risen* Lord and Savior that those women had before the resurrection. It means to love in your own way what they loved in the darkness. Let that be your guide.

From that point of view the strict weeks of Lent and then the severe demands of Holy Week make sense.

We have to prepare our souls to receive the tremendous gift of faith in the resurrection, and find all sorts of facets in ourselves to accept its fullness. We must be ready to let God fill up, drop by drop, the lamps of our souls with a priceless oil — without which everything is vain — which will make they burn with flames of generosity and patience. The control of the flame is up to us: it may flicker or blaze, grow or go out or remain to lighten the whole house.

At the Easter Vigil we hold candles in our hands, and they ask a clear question: Are your lamps ready for the light of Christ? Will the bridegroom find them so? Will you have provided oil and watched for his arrival, or will you have been one of the foolish ones? (Matt. 25).

The word *fidelity* has much to say to us. It implies the daily perseverant exercise of a humble faith. It is the only proper synonym of *True Faith*. Fidelity is "everyday faith": stubborn hopefulness, waiting and loving. Sometimes it seems as if the master of the house will never come; yet one believes that he will come, and we want everything to be ready and also to let him know that the house is redolent of thoughts of his absence. Our love wants him to know that we have been watching and eager for his promise, "If he comes in the second, or the third watch, and finds them so, blessed are those servants" (Luke 12, 38). Prepare for Easter as you prepare for eternity.

Each of you has her own way of preparing, corresponding to your varied anticipations of the bridegroom and the joys that he brings. He will call each by her own name: *"a name written which no man knows except himself"* (Apoc. 19, 12), or maybe simply "Mary," as he addressed Mary Magdalene in the garden. And each of you will find your own private word by which to address him: it will be a name that a loving and longsuffering heart discovers.

However, this preparation for Easter is not a solitary matter: we are far from being alone. The Vigil is lit by the glow of hundreds of candles, and Lent was marked by a host of children baptized and now awaiting the rich oil for their little lamps. We must not forget this. For when Easter Day arrives and the risen Christ says, *"Go to my brethren and say to them . . .",* we must have our brethren in mind and be ready to go to them. Our commission is no less than Mary Magdalene's and she was eagerest of all that our risen Savior be known and loved.

After Easter, another joy awaits us: it is the joy of knowing that we are called by the Lord whom we love so much to use our lamps to lead the way to the true light. Your lamps must burn brightly, for the road is dark.

Such — and so much more — is Paschaltide. Faith will lead us to explore it, and the Church's liturgy will help us to deepen the roots and understanding of our religion. Others as well as ourselves will rejoice.

WORK — I

"My Father works even until now, and I work" (John 5, 17). As usual with St. John, these words are not to be taken quite literally. They ricochet and have more than one significance.

The work of which Jesus speaks includes the mysterious process of creation, which continues to sustain the world and is the activity of the Word of whom St. Paul writes in his epistle to the Colossians: *"in him all things hold together."* There is also the redeeming work which continues down the ages throughout the world and touches each one of us in the form of a fatherly care. *"Not a hair of your head shall perish"* (Luke 21, 17). There is also our Lord's own mission whose events the gospels have recorded for us: the account of an agenda completed and climaxed by the cross. *"It is consummated"* (John 19, 30). God indeed works.

And we? Sloth takes a great many forms. There are a great many tasks imposed upon us — as many as there are personalities and temperaments. There is the laziness of those who do not want to get their hands dirty. There is the general physical sloth of over-methodical living, of taking it easy, being careful not to "overdo," mindful of one's health and careful to follow all the doctor's prescriptions. Fortunately there is always someone in a convent who never gets tired out, does not complain, neither thinks nor talks of her troubles — and everyone can lean on her! Péguy put it well when he spoke of "tireless human laziness."

It is true that we do not all have the same physical stamina. Nor the same courage.

Sloth is a vice and something to be dealt with. A religious

is by no means immune to it, for it is deeply rooted in human nature.

There is also spiritual and intellectual laziness, and it is a luxury that nuns cannot afford nowadays. They have the good fortune to be somewhat detached from the things that preoccupy the man in the street — the headlines, the speeches, the hit-songs of the radio, the whole merry-go-round of sight, sound, and words.

Use this freedom for work, for more than ever your faith needs to be clarified and enriched. A systematic plan of study will help each nun better to understand her faith and cultivate it, and make her more able to teach and communicate it. To be a catechist, for example, presupposes both intellectual work and the art of being a faithful religious. This is God's will and it is what the world needs.

It would be unthinkable for a community to fail to give its novices proper spiritual training and formation. The same must be said in respect to intellectual life. While it is true that one does not get rich through intellectual pursuits, their neglect is inexcusable.

Is it necessary to speak at all of spiritual sloth? We have been well enough warned of it. Do not fail to see that it often masquerades in the guise of physical or mental sloth.

When we say that God is always at work, are we not referring to the love of God? Because God loves us, he works. When indolence overcomes us in body or soul, let us have the courage to admit the real reason: we do not love God and his will enough. Love is strengthening and drives away sloth. As St. Augustine said, "When there is love, one does not talk of pain. Or, if there is pain, it is loved."

May God bless our work and give us strong hearts to do it, however hard or unaccustomed it may seem.

WORK — II

"... neither did we eat any man's bread at his cost, but we worked night and day in labor and toil, so that we might not burden any of you. Not that we did not have the right to do so, but that we might make ourselves an example for you to imitate us. For indeed when we were with you we used to charge you: if any man will not work, neither let him eat. For we have heard that some among you are living irregularly, doing no work but busy at meddling. Now such persons we charge and exhort in the Lord Jesus Christ that they work quietly and eat their own bread" (II Thess. 3, 8-12).

It is St. Paul who speaks, yet such words have echoes of today; someone might have addressed them to us in the street this morning.

Yesterday and today the emphasis on *work* has weighed on the pastoral conscience, sometimes so strongly that the Church has had to worry about people's sense of values, and particularly the value of the priesthood.

There is no doubt that public opinion considers a life which calls itself Christian but knows nothing of what St. Paul calls "labor and toil," neither a real nor respectable life. And they would lay the blame on Christ himself if he allows his religion and love to condone idleness, uselessness, or the exploitation of others.

In Pius XII's encyclical on the religious life, such an admonition underlies his references to old ideals and new departures in conventual life. It is well to reflect on this, both for enlightenment and for conscience's sake.

Poverty amounts to living off other people; that is what they say; it is not so, and we must let them know it. The really poor man works harder than anyone. And the poor people of God work harder. Nothing is clearer than the image shown us in the Gospels: Jesus, the Word-made-flesh, was poor and made a poor living by the work of his hands, a tiresome and tedious carpentry. He was a *workman*, his neighbors said, distinguishing him from one who wore a white collar or a blue one.

Of course there are and must be other than manual forms of work. St. Paul himself reminds us that his way of life was not obligatory but of his own choice (cf. I Cor. 9, 3-14) ; he claims the right that *"those who preach the Gospel should have their living from the Gospel."* For him, his real work was to preach Christ; the dangerous sea voyages and perils to life and health and reputation seemed only incidental. His mission was worth "work" of any sort.

There is always work to be done: circumstances, the common good, and one's own vocation determine what sort it may be. There is no place in the Church for idle people or dilettantes, especially not among those who aspire to perfection. It is up to each one of you, then, to see where the will of God lies and to determine the sort of work he wants you to do. Do not remain on the side-lines.

Simple and quiet organization of the religious life in a community which does not have to struggle for existence is a desirable but dangerous thing. It can lead to and encourage a certain nonchalance and indolence: "It is not urgent . . . there is always time . . . it will work itself out somehow . . . someone will help. . . ."

The days pass, the table is set, and one's conscience is clear. Worst of all, this blissful indolence reaches even to prayer — or so-called prayer which is nothing but day-dreaming. To while away the time on one's knees when some urgent work needs to be done or when obedience demands some unpleasant chore, can become an unholy abuse, provoking and irritating to others. Laziness in a community is a dreadful vice; and when it is hidden in the skirts of piety, it becomes a plague and sign of lack of vocation.

The time is short and there is not a moment to waste. What then must be done? What God asks, neither more nor less. He will never ask us to be idle: we will have all of eternity in which to rest. Busyness is not necessarily work, but idleness is a sin, especially under the cloak of religion, for it adds sacrilege as well. Let us be good workers in the Lord's vineyard, in peace and in truth.

LEISURE

Leisure hours! they belong to nuns as much as to the ordinary man, and are to be used well and properly. A Christian must learn to relax as well as to work and pray; he must allow himself leisure time and use it to the full. The ability to relax is a virtue in a real theological sense of the word.

In his *Introduction to the Devout Life*, which a nun ought to reread from time to time, St. Francis de Sales has some fine pages on the subject of relaxation as a facet of the virtue of charity. So even here in this slight matter, you see, we are in the realm of divine love.

Inability to relax can do much harm to a nun or a whole community. Normally, the rule or constitutions make provision for leisure time in the form of recreation, excursions, vacations, all of which must be given due and proper place in the life and not "denatured" or pushed aside by piety on the one hand or expediency on the other. Leisure time is not wasted time: on the contrary, it is very profitable time if it is real leisure.

Every religious ought to examine herself in this repect and consider whether her community really allows for leisure. Of course, it is the superiors' responsibility, yet each sister has a part in making "recreation" as important and refreshing as the word implies. And she must know how to relax.

Is it necessary to add that, while leisure must have its allotted time and not be displaced, one must be careful about the limits and manner of relaxation? It cannot be that of the ordinary person, although that is not to say that nuns may not enjoy relaxation.

In any community it is a most healthy and good sign when recreations are really refreshing and creative or when a nun chooses to spend some moments of leisure in reading, in taking a walk, or in silence. The whole of the spirit is involved; we learn this gradually and are finally won to the idea.

One loves God in leaning on his shoulder as well as in working for him, and he wishes it so.

Unhappily, this train of thought leads us to the world's idea of leisure and the poor pastimes with which our people content themselves. They are more than necessary to overworked and anxious men, yet they are so mundane and unrelated to any spiritual life that they are often questionable and sometimes disastrous.

In school work, for example, a nun ought to try to teach the children some sense of moderation in amusement, difficult as it may be, and show them the difference between play that is wild and exhausting and games that are healthy and fun.

There is a motto written in the hearts of many teachers,

"If I can hold out until Sunday...." There is deep and worthy feeling behind it, expressive of love for our Lord's work and confidence in his grace; however, it is the *Lord's* sabbath, and we must not put him aside with the work.

Pray for all sisters in school work. Pray also for those who stupidly spend their leisure in unwholesome and risky amusements. Pray for those in civic authority who have the duty and power to regulate public welfare. Without relaxation a man is lost; but through it he can lose his soul.

Pray for a proper observance of Sunday, that it may be a real day of rest and make God known and loved.

6

THE WORLD

THE APOSTOLATE, WORK OF GOD AND MAN

If the primary goal of the religious is the search for God and his perfection, there is another and not necessarily a secondary one: the apostolate. Let us give some thought to the consideration of the nature and demands of the apostolate.

Some of you are vowed to a contemplative life, but will surely gain from this, for no prayer is worthwhile apart from the Sacred Heart of our Lord, whose prayer was that we be apostles and missionaries.

To build up the Body of Christ

In Christ, perfection is two-fold. There is the inherent perfection of infinity and eternity. There is also the perfection of a created being, exemplified in the union of the Divine Word and the perfect man.

Yet Christ lacks perfection, a perfection of stature, of which St. Paul writes so profoundly. The mystical body, the Church, of which he is head and we its members, has not reached its full growth. Here on earth it stands unfinished, always "under construction." The full flourishing and final completion will not be seen until the end of time; however attached to the head the members may be by love and devotion, their relationship will be unsettled until the day of judgment.

That will be the day when the Church, the Body of Christ, and his Bride, reaches the fulfillment of her stature and beauty. Meanwhile, she will have produced and mothered many members by his grace, and they will have achieved their proper stature. Only then will the whole Body rejoice and sing an eternal *Te Deum*. Then the holy city, new Jerusalem, will have been built. Then the chosen people of God will have reached the promised land after the bitter years of wanderings; and, as the Messiah and Savior promised, they will enter the Kingdom of God.

Until then, it is a time for waiting and preparation — a time for the apostolate, time for the Body of Christ to increase. The Church, the new Eve and Bride of Christ, bears his children, Sons of God.

It is a time for the construction of Sion, the heavenly city. The Church gathers all men, living stones, chips and sculpts them to bring out their real beauty and fit them into the building of which Christ is both head and cornerstone.

It is a time for the people of God to march onward. Having left the land of bondage to sin, washed in the waters of baptism, there is a long exodus and, led by Christ our light, we trudge across the purifying desert of life. Such is the perspective that we must have if we are to view our apostolic task aright and understand its direction, demands and grandeur.

Individualism often causes us to limit our horizons to "our" projects, "our" children, "our" sick, forgetting that we work only in the name of the Church and for her as simple laborers in a grand project.

A Work of God

The apostolic mission is primarily and essentially a supernatural work. We are too easily tempted to forget that it is above all the divine work, the work of Christ.

The Goal

What is the goal of any apostolate? The ever greater glory of God. *"Hallowed be thy name, thy kingdom come, thy will be done...."* It was primarily for the Father's glory that Christ became incarnate: *"taking the nature of a slave ...obedient to death on a cross."*

The Church works, suffers and fights for the glory of God. Think what its apostolate has meant: the zeal of the apostles and missionaries, the blood of martyrs, the accomplishments of so many soldiers of Catholic action, and the efforts of all the people of God. From beginning to end, it is for the glory of God.

There are also, of course, souls to be rescued; yet this is all part of the same work and has no other purpose than God's glory. We save them only by giving them to God, and God to them.

The Theory

What is the goal of all apostolic work? To make men sons of God. To impart the divine life to mankind ever more abundantly. Yet, it is God alone who can do this, and it is the free gift of his love.

The goal is to bring men to the light and truth for which they are made, to allow them to become children of light, and to hand on to them the faith. Yet, God alone is the light and the truth, and only he can touch a soul to enlighten and give the gift of faith. The goal is deliverance from sin, the giving of pardon, purification and peace. Yet God alone forgives, and only he can purge a soul and fill it with his love and peace. The apostolate essentially means to give God to men, God who is love, life, light and peace. Only God can give himself — to whom he wills and when he wills, through the channels that he chooses, fully, freely. Let us not debase the apostolate to a matter of methods and human technique. "Unless the Lord build the house, they labor in vain who build it" (Ps. 126, *Nisi Dominus*).

The Means

The means must always be suitable to the end sought. No merely natural, human means can lead to an end that is in the supernatural order, and the apostolate is quite another thing than a program of techniques and methods. It does indeed make use of human means and techniques, but the mission itself is of another order, the order of grace. The supernatural means are those ordained and constituted by Christ himself in the Church: Prayer, which is efficacious insofar as it is the prayer of Christ. *"Ask, and it shall be given you. . . . Ask in my name." "If you had faith the size of a grain of mustard seed, you could move mountains." "This kind of devil is cast out only by prayer and fasting."* The revelation of the Word of God: the proclamations of the Gospel, the Good News. The more wholeheartedly and forcefully it is done, the more fruitful it will be. The apostle is only the herald and witness; what the world waits for and what we must offer is the Word of God, not our own poor words.

The evangelical virtues must be evident: *"You are the salt of the earth . . . you are the light of the world." "Let your light shine before men, in order that they may see your good works and give glory to your father in heaven."* Here are the proper supernatural signs of the work of grace in us.

Finally, the sacraments: outward signs of inward grace, beneficial because they are the action of the Christ and his Church.

A Work of Men

God needs men for his supernatural work of love. Having chosen the Incarnation for the restoration and redemption of creation, he has forever joined human nature with his own in his plan of salvation. So, truly tied to me, he is in a sense dependent upon them.

The Incarnate Word has united the whole of mankind with himself. Thus, a humanity sanctified by this union with the Word becomes a necessary and joint instrument of redemption and sanctification.

God needs us not only as objects of his love and grace, accepting them with an *Amen*, but also because he wishes to give himself to men through men. It is through them that he transmits his Word, his forgiveness, and all the graces we need. He committed his authority and sacraments into the hands of men.

He needs men of his own choice, whom he sends and

delegates, making them sharers in the work of his Son, who is his unique priest and apostle.

Apostles are such only by virtue of their participation in Christ's apostolate, united and identified with him and animated by his Spirit. They are such only as instruments joined with him, instruments as perfect as possible, disinterested, dedicated, and flexible in the hands of God.

The Perfect Instrument

Doubtless God can — and often does — work wonders through very imperfect instruments. But the better the instruments, the more easily he accomplishes his purpose. God's glory and man's salvation depend not simply upon the number of apostles, but on their quality.

Supernatural Perfection: The apostle is obligated by his office to seek ever greater perfection until he lives entirely by love of God. The more closely he is united to God in charity, the more freely God will be able to use him. No one can give what he does not have, so how can we offer the divine light, love, life or peace unless we live in him? The interior life is always the well-spring of the apostolic mission; the work, if it is anything, is its radiation and overflowing.

Natural Perfection: The apostle is a man who offers to God's service his own possibilities, gifts and human qualities. For the sake of the apostolate and for the Kingdom of God, we ought to desire to be humanly perfect, especially in intellectual matters and in the sphere of public relations.

A lively, cultivated mind, a reliable memory and clear judgment are invaluable. It is important to know how to hear and listen, observe and reflect in order to grasp, understand and solve problems presented.

The apostle should have keen sensibility but keep it under control. His heart should be generous and warm, understanding, open and friendly. He must develop and purify his ability to sympathize, for it is of utmost importance in the present dialogue with others. He must be strong-willed and able to surmount many obstacles and disappointments. And it is important that he be as sound as possible in body and spirit. Grace does not suppress nature, but rather uplifts and perfects it and makes it useful. Nature is not to be despised, but to be put to God's service; and the finer it is, the better he can use it.

A Joint Instrument

As apostles, we are only instruments in the hands of God, and as such, let us keep our place. However perfect, the instrument is valuable only insofar as it is "pliable" by the master. As apostles, we must place ourselves in God's hands and let him work what he pleases; he will accomplish this if we are supple, docile, self-given, and disinterested. It is our part to let him act in and through us, letting him take the initiative, and offering him all the attentiveness and docility that grace makes possible.

FAITH IN THE LAITY

One is inclined to be suspicious of an impetuous spirit, lest it not be mated with real generosity. We must be willing to understand and to reflect, and this is often — indeed, almost always — harder than spending ourselves in some other way. We prefer to give ourselves immediately, without stopping to consider how best to do so. This is manifestly irrational and therefore not good. At bottom, there must be some laxity and lack of generosity hidden away.

For this reason, no one dares ignore the enormous effort of the Church today in respect to the souls of the laity. Can a nun fail to see and consider this? How could she refuse to reflect on it and the ways in which she might cooperate with the will of the Church?

In this sphere, as in every other that concerns the Kingdom of God, a nun's profession and dedication create possibilities, demands and duties. Can she shrink from them?

The secular life is not hers; nor is it her vocation. However, just as the laity ought to understand and appreciate the unique value of the Religious Life, so the Religious must understand and appreciate the immense value of the layman's vocation.

Pius XI stated in unforgettable terms that the Church considers it a real gift of grace that in our times there has been an awakening of apostolic spirit in those who are neither priests nor religious. Coming at a time when reduction in the Church's means and resources, together with an increase in needs, was leading to discouragement, there was this new blossoming of what seem limitless possibilities, as if a great fortune were put in our hands. There is a shortage of priests; there are not enough Religious; and above all, neither the one nor the other is close enough to the realities of the world that needs conversion and renewal! Yet, there are all the baptized in whom Christ lives and acts and who, by their situation in the world, are at the very heart of things.

It is no exaggeration to liken this awakening of a lay apostolate to the recent discovery of atomic energy. The coal mines are nearly empty, the power drawn from mountain rivers and dams is becoming insufficient . . . suddenly, right at hand, is the unsuspected and limitless power of a tiny atom.

The use of this spiritual resource has only just begun.

Our Sisters, ever more attentive than anyone to the Kingdom of God, ought to be touched by this new light, stirred up by its hope, and determined to serve its cause.

Believe in the apostolic roles of those who are neither priests nor Religious: Christian families; Christian workers, rich and poor; adults or children. Believe in it sincerely and strongly enough to be collaborators in a powerful and effective Catholic action. Be willing to understand movements which sometimes have a disconcerting form, to participate in them as candidly as is fitting, and try to learn how to assist them. It is on these conditions that our prayers are sound and effective. It cannot harm a nun whose conscience is in good order, involved and alive to the proper mission of the Religious.

The day when our priests succeed in training militant laymen and setting real Catholic action in motion; the day when the apostolic spirit bestowed in baptism arouses men's hearts, in that day there will be no more problem of recruitment: there will be plenty of priests.

The day when nuns have fully entered into every domain of their work, whether in education or elsewhere, there will be no more problems of recruiting. A Church more alive will produce its fruits in abunance, particularly that exquisite fruit which is vocation to a life of perfection.

THIS STRANGE WORLD

The life of today is constantly pushing us to the brinks of chasms, and we turn away in dizziness. The present world whirls at a tremendous pace, like an automobile driven at full speed over a road famous for accidents. It reaches precipices beyond which all seems to disappear, hangs in space for a moment by a miracle, swerves and veers on. At one minute the passengers' heads are turned upward to the sky, then suddenly they are directed down to the ground which seems to fall away into depths as infinite as the sky.

It is impossible for anyone to get away from it or ignore it and isolate oneself: a thousand voices echo the distant rumblings of the future and we hear the heavy sounds of storms to which none of us is a stranger.

What becomes of the Gospel in all this? Amid the clamor of words and threats and cries, what is the good news? Where are we, with our faith and our Christ?

Such questions cannot but arouse anguish in all of us.

Millions appear to be cut off from us; whole nations of people have given themselves, body and soul, to a mighty and crushing movement which wipes out their independence along with their anxieties; they have chosen the destiny of being blind servants and cogs in a great machine. We cannot look without shuddering at the Chinese hordes or the Russian people ... those hundreds of millions for whom Christ died.

The least of these is our brother under the love of God, who gave them life only in order to assure of another, eternal life, and who placed them in this world only for the day when they might know the unshadowed and endless joy of the glory of the Lord. What a mystery!

No one expects to find the answer to this secret; but the secret makes inescapable demands. We were not born to *see*, at least not in this life, but to believe. And it is our faith that sustains the world, a faith that soars high in the realms of hope and charity — our faith with its daily humble submission and its prayer and fervor for the Kingdom of God.

Unfathomably, on this faith hangs the salvation of countless unknown men and women near and far, lost in the crowd and apparently determined to lose themselves, yet who are never absent from the Mind of God. Once a slave was sold like a chattel, but God let him know how precious he was through the letter of Saint Paul to Philemon. Yesterday a slave, today a man among the masses, type of millions plodding and toiling, he is part of the providential mystery, and we believe that God speaks to him.

We are not called upon to know or unravel the secrets of the world and of time; we are called to know and love Christ, who created the world and is the author of its history.

Never has the Gospel rung out more clearly. Never have we felt more surely that, despite revolutions, its words are eternal. If they had *not* been the wisdom of the world, they would have long ago become meaningless and become a thing of one or another epoch past.

Actually, there is no comparison between the light of the Gospel and the lights of the world. The latter can be bright, even dazzling, for they belong to divine creation; but the Word of God is spoken from a higher than human level, and although it is *for* and *in* the world, it is not *of* the world. To win the world is not a dream forbidden to man, but one can win the world and lose his life. This is the mystery of the Gospel and of the Incarnation.

The mysteries of history are challenges to our faith, not our thought. Unhappy and fruitless reflections are not for us, but a courageous effort to persevere according to the Gospel. So many signs, within and without, show us that its words do not pass away.

Nineteen hundred years ago a man disembarked at Puteoli, the port of Rome and of the Empire. He was alone. At Athens, the scornful philosophers had made him sweat; but he carried Christ in him. His name was Paul.

What Christ did then, he continues to do now. Today, each of us is Paul.

May God give us the faith and with it the desire to communicate it, and then we will not lose it.

A faithful Religious — how beautiful she is in the eyes of God, and then in the sight of those who seek for goodness.

In this present world, when the mystery weighs so heavily, may God keep you for this urgent mission and lead you to accept it thankfully. That is my prayer.

WHAT IS "THE WORLD"?

When one reads the Gospel as it should be read, desiring to take the divine words seriously, one sometimes pauses abruptly at some passage in our Lord's sayings, as if it were new — as if one had never really grasped it before. It is like a doorway that one has passed hundreds of times without entertaining the notion of its opening.

There are always excuses for this sort of inattention: no one around us seems to take biblical study very seriously, and to do so would be to become involved in too many problems.

Whatever the reason, we consign whole sections of the Gospel's teaching to oblivion, and then some day find that they are disastrously missing from our interior make-up.

Recently people talked of a sort of universal consent-by-silence in respect to this or that disbelief —"Who talks of Hell anymore . . . or Purgatory . . . or the Devil?" And the silence amounts to a "negative heresy."

One rarely speaks any more of "the world"— that world which our Lord so strongly opposed. You may be sure that that world profits by the silence to regain its place surreptitiously in our hearts and even our souls. This applies even to those men and women who have renounced the world not only as do all baptized Christians, but further the advantages and security of worldly life in the belief that they are but obstacles to the goal to which faith calls.

Today there are interesting and compelling reasons to reread our Lord's invectives against "the world." Whom did he include? What could justify such threats and anger on his part? As for ourselves, do we understand his indignation? Are there traces in us of such passionate impatience? The truth is that nowadays we settle with the world, and carry on a sort of flirtation with it, overlooking its hostilities or putting up with them. We speak, read, look, listen, and give ourselves indifferently, as if anything could be said, read, seen, heard or given without harm.

Where does the "world" begin? One thing to notice is that the frontiers if there are any at all-have become very vague.

It will be a worthwhile exercise for you to return to the gospel and our Lord's words about the world, question their meaning, and also yourselves. Does there exist for you, friends of Christ, a *hateful* world which you can oppose?

Every profession includes this question; hear its echoes. Hatred of the world and charity are two sides of the same coin, and the one is the measure of the other. Think on this.

May the Holy Spirit guide you, so that the Church can count on the benefits of your fidelity.

CURRENT EVENTS

In the world today, the air is filled with noise and reports of all sorts: the sounds invade every Cloister. We must accept it, but try not to be its victims.

Flight is no solution, for the invasion spreads everywhere, and there are no barriers to its innundations. Events and news then plague us even more.

Much of the clamor is a "distraction" which we cannot entirely shut out of our prayers; it is of the sort that we chase out the door, only to have it return by the window. If we cannot completely rid ourselves of it, there is a certain freedom to be found in simply putting up with it.

The affairs of the present world involve everyone, even the most completely withdrawn of nuns.

This is the way it is, and we must accept it.

For example, the Carmelites vote. Thus, they play their part in the future of their country and take a responsibility for the common good — for religion and morality are at stake. Willingly or unwillingly, they are cogs in the machinery; it is only a question knowing what decisions to make and why. Therefore, they keep informed. So, there they are in the movement, along with the others.

Let us be frank. Is this much different from former days? In one way or other, one heard what was going on, and one knew lots of things. The word "parlor" has not lost its root meaning.

Perhaps the present situation merely demands that one be better-informed and understand better the import of the news.

Maybe now we will become more aware that a *discipline of information* exists and we ought conscientiously to adapt ourselves to it. It is no longer a choice between knowing or not knowing, but between accurate or inaccurate knowledge, between vague and unreliable information and that which is sure. We are no longer free simply to watch things run their course.

So, I am willing to say that communities ought to have clear and precise rules about such matter — rules which are not merely negative, for that would be a mistake. What we do not learn from its proper source, we will find out through unreliable channels.

Such rules are not hard to outline, although they are less easily carried out, for they require tact and patience, and each sphere of the Community has its own needs — e.g., they apply differently to active and cloistered nuns.

First: one must learn to be shrewd. In the flood of news, not everything is worth knowing. There are some things that ought to be known. As for the rest, which are not worthwhile, we must learn systematically to brush them aside.

There are some newspapers that a nun ought not to read and magazines that she ought not to read, because they are useless. In those that she may or ought to read, there are things that she ought to skip over, lest they hinder God's work in her soul. It is a matter of honesty on her part. In one form or another, this discipline is for everyone, but it should be rigorous in those who have chosen God alone.

Lurid stories of crimes are not God's only competitors, but they are dangerous ones and to be avoided.

Second: one must know how to make use of what one learns, and this is rather difficult and complex. It has at least two aspects: one must be critical and not simply devour the news, and one must also try to make use of it for the glory of God in oneself, one's work, and in the Community.

This will invite many remarks and be interpreted in many ways. Let us remember that one of the chief counsels of wisdom is to be silent. To talk of the news generally means to be uncritical and to let it command our attention and take it from our Lord, our prayer, our love and our work.

Such remarks will seem strange. Yet, thinking them over, devout and sincere souls will wonder that they had not occurred to them sooner. To be content with God is not merely an ideal but a possibility.

7

TRIALS AND PROMISES

THE CROSS

Every action and understaking, every life that is good and beautiful and truly Christian, bears the double sign of love and sacrifice. These two things resemble and symbolize the cross. One cannot do without the other, or it is not the cross.

However, natural instinct tends to reject, or at least to gloss over and make us forget the second of those elements. We are glad to love, but we do not want to suffer. It is a good thing to recognize that such an interior exists, hidden, ceaseless and inevitable.

We must warn ourselves of deceptions and delusions. Our love now may be strong and sincere enough for us to think suffering normal and even desirable. But a day will come when this confidence weakens or collapses; then it will need all our faith to put together the two pieces of the cross and accept the fact that love and suffering are inseparable on this earth.

That is why the cross must always be our resort, "a lamp shining in a dark place." There at the cross, and only there, to love means to suffer; there, we understand that it is necessary, and accept it.

Trials and suffering, when they arise, will always strike us as extraordinary, shocking and undeserved, especially when they happen at a time when we are happily and generously devoted (cf. I Peter 4, 12-17).

We lose sight of the Christ. With whom were we in love? Jesus or someone else? Jesus crucified? There is no other.

To keep one's eyes on the cross is the only way to keep from being surprised, or at least to survive the shock and return to reality.

To suffer without loving is sub-human and leads to passive resignation or giving up to despair. If it is sub-human, it is even less Christian. Suffering is only a part of the wood of the cross. On the cross is the crucified one, and this is a matter of love.

Even in consecrated lives, alas, suffering can detach itself from the cross and become a matter of the soul's gnawing on itself, shut up with its malady as with an executioner.

One does not reason with suffering, nor argue. It is related to sin and is the result of it; yet it can become the enemy of sin if love is equal to it, surmounts it, and by it, like Jesus, reaches the beloved Father through the light of the Christ and the assurance of resurrection.

There is a spiritual hygiene for physical or mental suffering: it is to call it by its right name taught us by faith — sacrifice. It is a bit of the cross, a bit of the great saving Sacrifice. Suffering never mentions its name. When it comes, it says nothing: it only hurts. But faith speaks the true name and helps us to believe that the suffering is right and a real communion with our Redeemer. Thus, it is less a cross than *his* cross.

When suffering is an act of love, one can never take offense or be overwhelmed by it. Indeed, its most repellent forms will be the truer ones, the worthier to be called a cross — the most unjustified ones, those that reach deepest. These best resemble the cross of our Lord.

We must tell ourselves this daily, for each day makes us forget it.

No one can say he realizes it all, for the cross, like Jesus, is revealed anew every day. But it is *he* who is there, and with the shock, there is the hidden, promised joy of an encounter with one who does not deceive.

Come, Lord Jesus.

"WHAT IS LACKING OF THE SUFFERINGS OF CHRIST" (Col. 1, 24)

Trials always dismay us, "as if something strange were happening," undue and unusual (cf. I Peter 4, 12).

Our deep and heavy need for tranquillity is disconcerted by shocks, and something in us objects to being tested. Despite ourselves, we resist trials. From there it is easy to go on, accepting the trial with poor grace, and regard it as a contradiction of God's goodness. We get over one trial, but the next one finds us again shocked and dismayed. For there is always another.

"Yet God is good." Yes, God is good. His name is Jesus Christ, and we believe it.

We shall never accept the bad. Fortunately, something in us will always protest, and our natures, warped and sinful though they may be, fight against evil. God does not ask us to accept evil. He asks us only to agree that his name is Jesus Christ.

We have false ideas of grace. Grace is not given to harden our hearts. It is not meant to take away our aspira-

tions to joy and happiness. "Happy are you . . . ," said our
Lord in the sermon on the Mount. Rather, grace is the
Creator's signature to the happiness meant for us, the assurance of our hopes, and the conditioner of all existence
and activity.

Grace is not for stoics. It does not make us insensitive;
on the contrary, it makes us more and more sensitive as it
pours into us the tenderness of love. Grace causes us to love.
Since love has a hard mission to accomplish in us and in
the world as it is; since it cannot find its way to us and the
world until it *"has broken down the intervening wall"* (Eph.
2, 14), with violent assault on the weakest points (cf. Matt.
11, 12; 12, 29); in other words, since we ourselves are incapable of loving God and man as truly, strongly and
lastingly as we ought, grace has given us Jesus Christ to
love (cf. John 6, 44).

We do not love suffering. If we did, it would be absurd,
abnormal, and contrary to God's plan. By ourselves, we are
unable to love God or our brethren in sincerity and truth;
therefore, he has given us Jesus Christ in whom we find
both and with whom we can approach and overcome our
troubles. Our troubles then are not merely sufferings —
which cannot and ought not to be loved — when they become ways of loving Christ. The protests of nature in us will
not be quiet, but the love of Christ will speak louder. That
is all.

"I shall never be able to love ordeals." A mistaken ambi-
tion, for an ordeal is never amiable. "My love is not strong
enough to be put to the test. . . ." Who asks that it should
be? "I shall never succeed in loving others enough to overcome the endless trials they present." Are we the measure
of brotherly love?

Instead of trying to love suffering, or straining to love God, or stretching to love our neighbors, what if one fine day we gave ourselves simply to loving Jesus Christ?

Far from becoming insensitive, we should still have found the door to God, the only one always open and welcoming. *"I am the door"* (John 10, 7).

We are not to love trials, but to love to follow Christ, even if it means suffering. We are not asked to support our troubles with joy, but to walk joyfully in the steps of Christ, carrying his Cross (cf. Matt. 9, 20).

God is infinitely lovable, but can our hearts ever meet that end? Jesus is infinitely lovable, and our hearts can reach his and find God there.

Suffering is not lovable, but Jesus who suffers is, and we can love him when his suffering becomes ours.

Brotherly love is always costly and never idyllic; it is a struggle never won for ourselves and demanding great sacrifice. *"We likewise ought to lay down our life for the brethren"* (I John 3, 16). But Jesus, our elder brother (cf. Romans 8, 29), is for us uniquely and perfectly lovable; and in and with and like him, we can help our brethren until the end.

No, we do not lack resources; it is just that we use them poorly. There is nothing wrong with our guns and ammunition, but we do not see the target. Who can truthfully say that she is incapable of loving Christ by the grace of God?

"By him and with him and in him" all things are possible and are promised. How much real force is wasted on objectives that are imaginary or inaccessible. How much effort is spent on quixotic combats and unreal problems. *"Only one thing is needful"* (Luke 10, 42), so it is possible: to love God with all your might, and your neighbor as yourself. To achieve this, there is one road: Jesus our Savior, to whom, with open and ready hearts, we refuse nothing. Blessed is she who has been mysteriously called to have no other care than Jesus Christ (cf. I Cor. 7, 32). Blessed is she if she weighs her treasure, the only one that cannot be counterfeit, that no one can steal, and is inexhaustible: *"Christ's love which surpasses knowledge ... that you may be filled unto all the fullness of God"* (Eph. 3, 19).

CHRIST'S TRIUMPH

For us it is and always will be hard to avoid separating Christ's triumph from his work, passion and death. We share his sufferings, unite our thoughts and prayers to his Passion, and then at other times feel ourselves sharers of the glorious joy of the resurrection; but these two communions, so to speak, remain independent, as if they were not really related. Yet they are related, and the one is implicit in the other. The passion is only for the sake of the resurrection. The resurrection is from the tomb, where the passion and death led our Savior.

Throughout the pains and trials of his mortal life, our Lord never ceased to anticipate victory, *"watching Satan fall from heaven"* (Luke 10, 17), *"lifted up from the earth, I will draw all things to myself"* (John 3, 32). Those are the reasons for his humiliation and destiny; without them, it would have been completely absurd for the Son of God to take human nature upon him and humble himself to the death of the Cross (cf. Phil. 2, 6).

"Now my soul is troubled ... Father, save me from this hour. No, that is why I came to this hour. Father, glorify

thy name. . . . Now will the prince of the world be cast out . . ." (John 12, 27-31).

This is he who triumphed and arose from the grave and returned to men, leading captivity captive (Col. 2, 15). This is he who breathed his last gasp on the Cross amid the tauts of his enemies and the dismay of his friends. He who shows himself to his disciples is the Man with scarred hands and wounded side, and by these marks he is recognized. *"He has taken the decree against us completely away, nailing it to the Cross"* (Col. 2, 14).

The Christian life finds its true balance only when this mystic unity has been discovered — rather, when it has been accepted. The balance lies in not breaking this strong union which, on the one hand, ties all true joy in Christ to his passion, and, on the other, allows the flame of faith (now become sure hope) to pierce the darkness of all our trials and troubles.

It is a mysterious and aching alliance — this between life and death, suffering and joy. Only the friends of Christ who are determined *not* to leave him and who cling to his promise (cf. John 6, 68-69) are capable of maintaining these ties and living in the half-light which is that of the faith.

To enjoy the light of the world as if the world's life were the true light, to forget that sooner or later it will be clouded over. To accept pain or desolation simply as one of the hard parts of existence and await its end, although it certainly will end only at death. Many people live this way, even Christians. It is not the way of truth nor of Christ. The one who loves sees things otherwise.

Yes, how many Christians live as if Christ had not come and when trouble arrives, they are as men without hope (I Thess. 4, 12); or when things go well, they act as if the joys of this world were never to pass away (I Cor. 7, 31).

Let me repeat: only a direct relationship with our Lord, only deliberate and absolute trust in his word, and only his love can give us the power to overcome our instinctive natural reactions. At best, what can nature do but bear a malady and wait until it passes, as one takes shelter during a thunderstorm, and then rejoice if luck is good. All that is human. But it is not true. Thank God, we have a better way. We know, thank God, that we are not condemned to being *"tossed to and fro and carried about by every wind"* (Eph. 4, 14) or fruitless suffering or joy that is soon spent. It is enough that we are *"looking towards the author and finisher of faith, Jesus, who for the joy set before him, endured a Cross, despising the shame"* (Heb. 12, 1). The light that does not fail comes only from that direction.

This is all so contrary to our natural impulses and so seems beyond our powers, that there must be found in the world some souls close enough to Jesus and confident enough in his Word to demonstrate that it is possible.

If hearts vowed to his love and marked by a special vocation are not setting this example, then who will do it? *"Do you also wish to go away?"* (John 6, 68): this burning question that our Lord asked his disciples cannot leave us unmoved.

It is not a question of our developing great virtues or resources; on the contrary, it is a matter of our surrendering unreservedly to a power greater than ours, a strength that is in fact made perfect in our weakness (cf. II Cor. 12, 9-10).

Perhaps the final word to scatter the clouds of our semi-good will is humility. A humility based on faith, wishing to receive everything from God, light as well as strength; a humility which calls us to follow Jesus, walking in his steps, doing only what he does. Would this not be true love? (cf. Mark 8, 34).

This is the lesson that the world so very much needs, or rather the lesson that Jesus wishes to teach the world, through us, to save it. *"Was not our heart burning within us when he was speaking . . ."* (Luke 24, 32).

"So that I may know him and the power of his resurrection and the fellowship of his sufferings: become like to him in death, in the hope that somehow I may attain to the resurrection . . ." (Phil. 3, 10-11).

May that be your wish and dearest desire, in order that his Kingdom may come.

THE PEACE OF CHRIST

"Peace be with you . . . I give you my peace . . . blessed are the peacemakers . . . Be at peace among yourselves."

Peace! Few words in the Gospel bear such hope or fall more happily on our ears.

The abuse of it for propaganda's sake serves only to emphasize the place it has in our hearts.

The thought of our Lord, as well as the teaching of the Church, gives a comprehensive meaning to the word. What we must want, as Christians, is peace in its ordinary, every-day meaning of harmony and accord among men, without strife or violence, and above all, without war. Above and beyond this, there is peace in a profounder sense: it is the condition of the existence of peace among men, born of a good conscience, where hearts and desires are dominated by charity; in short, it is the gift of Christ.

St. John's vision of the City of Peace at the close of the Apocalypse includes the light of the Lamb, universally shared, with no more tears or sorrow.

The scene before our eyes today is something else. We are haunted by the dreadful spectre of war, and the echoes of cannon, near and far, never cease. We dare not think, indeed, we hardly can, of the possibilities of nuclear warfare.

Meanwhile, nothing is sadder or more bitterly cruel and implacable than the struggles that are going on in society and even taking the form of civil wars, quietly smoldering, and now and then bursting into flames at our very gates and in our streets. The battles are fought also in long newspaper columns, billboard posters, and deep in men's hearts. Whether it is a matter of defiance or hatred, action or omission, this sort of war is the heaviest and least tolerable burden for a Christian.

The least tolerable! Nevertheless, we adjust ourselves to it in hundreds of ways that are more or less hypocritical, more or less dishonest.

The class struggle can be exploited; or one can condemn it and still profit by it.

At the base of all these hostilities and strife, and the explosive impatience, there has been and there is something that rests in every human heart and which our Lord denounced with great vehemence: the love of money. Money is the most shameful of idols — the most sordid, the unworthiest, the most sacrilegious of God's rivals. It provokes the most abject and inexcusable crimes, and is the lowest form of slavery to which a man can give himself.

God or mammon: one must choose which of the two

masters to serve. A compromise is impossible. If the masses hate one another, if great nations around the world are in a permanent state of war, with its attendant evils, it is money that is at the bottom of it, and money is to be blamed for what is unjust in their systems. We must toss this idol out of our hearts. Nothing that right and justice lead us to construct will bring peace so long as money is God. The idol must be smashed in each of us, for the voice of Christ continues to resound, to call us away from an everlastingly menacing danger.

The vow of poverty does not make one immune to temptation. One's heart is always ready for the joy of possessing, the desire to have, the pleasure of material assurance. The evil assumes many forms, the love of money rises up wearing a thousand masks, and the noblest and most "community-minded" are not the least among the deceivers.

The devil flees from the gaze of a child, says St. Thérèse of Lisieux. The dreadful idol that keeps the world enslaved and destroys peace, this mammon, can crumble under the gaze of one of Christ's truly poor.

The veiled fidelity of the poor and humble nun can do more for justice and peace between the classes than can economic systems and social contracts. *"Blessed are the poor in spirit . . . blessed are the peacemakers."* They are one and the same.

PEACE

Few words touch our hearts so deeply today as does this one.

Few words are so badly exploited.

Our Lord took care to warn against deception: it is peace of a certain sort, his sort, that he gives. *"My peace I leave with you ... not as the world giveth ..."* (John 14, 27).

The peace of Jesus! Are we always quite sure that we are thinking and talking of *that* peace? Is it his peace that we long for? Do we seek to serve as peacemakers in the sense in which he ordered it in his Sermon on the Mount? We must do so to be worthy of the name of Children of God. Around us, alas, peace is a great question. We must not be indifferent to the deep and vital longings of men around us.

Except to a few wretchedly insane people, war is hateful. It is easy not to think of the wars of others which do not threaten us. But we must remember the atrocious misery that belongs to wars and not fail to share the pain of all those whom war crushes, mutilates, displaces and scatters around the world.

The Church prays for the peace which ends war.

Not all peace is Christian. The peace of the world can mean the silence of the dead, the oppression of the weak, and the ruin of the conquered land. This sort of peace breeds wars. True peace cannot be made by men of ill will. It must be made with justice, and justice always demands sacrifice.

A Christian who seeks peace will do well to ask himself if it is this sort of peace that he has been wishing and working for. The world lacks the peace that has been driven out of it by constant gunfire: what peace there is, is unstable and explosive. The very same situation can be found inside an ordinary family house!

Our Lord came to bring peace to mankind, as we sing in the *Gloria in excelsis*. He wished this peace to remain in every home he visited, and charged the apostles to speak peace in his name to every house that welcomed them. Yet there are Communities where peace does not reign. And there are some where peace which is not true peace reigns.

How can one tell? It is quite simple: the only true peace is that of Jesus, which dwells in him and which he imparts.

Is it necessary to describe this peace? St. Paul does so, beautifully: *"the fruit of the Spirit is charity, joy, peace, patience, kindness, goodness, faith, modesty, continency"* (Gal. 5, 22). It is a sort of procession, and peace walks only in the company of all her sisters.

They are the conditions in which one may live peaceably, and peace vanishes if her companions are taken away. Or, what remains under the name of peace is an illusion.

This explains why peace is precarious and difficult. And nothing shows better that true peace is a divine gift. In each person's heart, peace expects to find steady courage. In each house, she rests upon the common courage. Finally, in the world, it is useless to look for her apart from sacrifice and love.

May our Lord indwell each of your houses, which is his own, to say, Peace be with you. The real peace.

CONCLUSION

INTEGRATION OF THE RELIGIOUS INTO THE DIOCESAN PROGRAM

The religious life and religious institutes have to find their way in a difficult world. Even the efforts of daily *life* in such a world can make them lose sight of their *raison d'être*, and they end by no longer wondering or questioning it. This is sometimes the fault of outsiders who make impossible and inappropriate demands upon the Sisters, but the trouble can also lie within the Community.

The religious life is a divine summons: so, to begin with, an act of faith is necessary in order to discern the vocation. Faith alone leads us to a right estimate of religious vocation and its particular exercise. Consider the new aspirant: she evidently has no clear ideas about the life or her place in it, and she thinks of becoming a nun as someone else might seek a position in social work. Are we not sometimes responsible for this illusion? Maybe even guilty of it?

So it is important to keep in mind that it is essentially a matter of God's absolutely free choice, a choice for which no one else is accountable.

When we try to explain religious vocation to people who do not understand it, we are inclined to make concessions, to descend to a merely human level of argument.

People want excuses for the religious life rather than explanations, or we imagine so. Nuns are useful because there are abandoned babies to be cared for; and there are the sick — and women have always devoted their lives to Christian service in hospitals, etc. But, if social progress and state welfare programs relieve us of such work (and they surely will), what will we be able to say? That we are out on a limb?

The religious life is to be definitely explained as a call to love God exclusively and to be loved by him alone in permanent agreement, dependent upon his grace.

The foundation of the religious vocation is certain faith in a God whose love for us knows no bounds. We find this love primarily at the Cross, whence it extends to his choices over the years of certain men and women to become his very own.

The religious life is not impressive unless one considers the vows. Without poverty, obedience and chastity, it melts away. The man in the street does not see all that. Nuns are now what he would call "poor people"; their vow of obedience has little meaning to him; chastity is incredible.

So, one must constantly return to that first certainty: *it has pleased the love of God to choose us* ... in order that we may live exclusively for him ... counting on that, we preferred to withdraw from all else.

Examine yourselves regularly in respect to these fundamental things: is every effort made to keep the vows of poverty, obedience, and chastity, which are the signs and seals of love, for these attachments can sometimes prove false.

Do ordinary people class us among "the poor"? One hesitates to answer. We ought to be so. If being "poor" means having a permit to beg and owning nothing as an individual, while the *Community* has all its needs, we are speechless — for the answer is *No*.

The man in the street might also despise the vow of chastity if it amounts to no more than life without a mate and produces a hardness of personality or lack of feminine graciousness. To be chaste does not mean to be heartless, but the contrary.

As for obedience, it is more than an inclination to obey or a passive conformity, for it must be an action of the will. It is an effort that often creates great interior tension, but often blossoms out (personally and commonly) into all sorts of creative activity through which the love of God is expressed. Throughout the Church's history, the daring works of charity have been born of obedience not apart from it. Obedience is not a paralysis.

Let us hope that unenlightened outsiders do not look on us as evil; at least, let us not give them any reason to think so.

Integration of the religious into the diocesan program. This title means, first, the presence in the diocese of nuns and their works, ruled over by love for God, poverty, obedience and chastity. Then there are the details of putting them and their vows to work.

Through her experience and traditions, the Church has given material aid to all who would abandon themselves to the divine love, and so produced the Communities where the religious life could happily flourish.

Given those circumstances, it is now the place of each one to find her place in the pastoral life of this portion of the Church which is a diocese.

(This parenthesis is a bit daring: the Rule is, to see what the Church wishes.)

The bishop is not a potentate: the Church has described his limits and told him how he should behave and what he ought to do about his Sisters. The origin of a religious vocation gives it a real autonomy. The Church gives some rights to bishops and withholds others: she tells a bishop his responsibilities and of what place nuns ought to have in his apostolate.

The bishop's administrative duties have been greatly reduced: he is rather the witness and agent of your spirit. It is not his place to intrude some new spirit, but rather to help you to be faithful to your own, believing, respecting and developing it. Your bishop is trying to become acquainted with the ideals of each community and to make the most of them. He will not push them in some direction which is not theirs.

Constitutions and rules exist to govern and guide our religious orders. Just as one does not pull at a plant to make it grow, so the bishop, as a gardener, merely supplies the water without which the sap does not properly rise. It is the sap which is the life of the plant, and the bishop does not provide that.

The bishop of a diocese has a dual role in respect to his Sisters. As far as he is able, he must give them faith in the role they play; for they are irreplaceable, and their disappearance would be a loss of great power to the Church.

The bishop must also do all he can to make known his own pastoral outlook and program, for all sorts of possibilities await the employment of all sorts of gifts and talents. Well from within, God makes the sap rise. The bishop must determine the direction that the apostolic work is to take in the diocese, as far as he can rightly judge; and it is up to him to invite you to join in it.

It is the bishop who outlines the pastoral organization and its goals according to what he believes best for today's changing scene. He points directions and fixes ultimate goals rather than immediate objectives, then he mobilizes the best troops he has for the work.

Obviously, intense efforts are demanded for the diocesan work of today. To avoid overlapping and waste, all resources must be coordinated. In one field, there are too many workers; in another, none at all. Situations change and we are slow to adapt to them.

The general episcopal policy in this country is to let each one work in his or her own way and vocation, providing only that each one gives full measure and that everything that can be done *is* done.

THE NUN AND THE MISSIONS

Can one be a Religious and not a missionary? Certainly not. At least, a nun cannot refuse to give her thoughts and prayers to her missionary sisters at home and abroad.

Many institutions which were not originally founded for missions have long ago heard their call and responded. Thus, many Communities, indeed nearly all, are in constant touch with overseas missions, and fervently follow the work of grace in people being evangelized and the work of their sisters given to the service of this grace.

Are they less missionaries because their lot or health or circumstances keep them on this side of the oceans? Their hearts are no less fervent, their charity is real, and their interest is efficacious. In many cases, the merits of a real sacrifice are added to their generosity.

Even where the particular vocation of a Community precludes the undertaking of missionary work, who will doubt that the Church's urgent appeal echoes deeply in the hearts of those who have sincerely and completely exchanged their interests for Christ's?

At this point, it seems necessary to ask the Religious, whatever her vocation or work may be, to think and believe herself to be a real missionary.

If she is not one by virtue of the sphere in which she is working, she must be one by virtue of her accord with the heart of our Lord and by her special sharing of the divine love, *"who wishes all men to be saved"* (I Tim. 2, 4), and who is constantly sending us in search of his own: *"Other sheep I have who are not of this fold. Them also I must bring"* (John 10, 16).

If she does not see the task accomplished by her own hands, or if she lacks the joy of caring for the sick or opening the eyes of children in a missionary land, let her at least believe that her desire is not unimportant in the sight of God. Let her know that in some foreign field a priest or a missionary sister watches with gratitude over the blossoming of flowers whose seeds were blown from afar, confided to the winds of grace by a generous hand.

Every nun ought often to re-read some of St. Thérèse's simple and fervent pages where she speaks of her missionary aspirations and her certainty of God's knowledge of them. A nun will re-read them not to accuse herself of coldness or merely to kindle her zeal, but rather to estimate what she can do by virtue of her religious state. Let her not hesitate to devote her thoughts and imagination to the far-off lands where the Gospel has not yet taken root or borne fruit. Let pity fill her heart for poor creatures with souls made for better things, tortured by superstitious fears, ignorant of the truths that makes us proud to be men and happy to be Christians.

Nowadays it is so easy to visit these countries in spirit: yesterday they were so distant, and today but a few hours flight from this country. Imagine! There they still live in fear of demons, practice odious rites, and are criminally used and abused. Yes, they exist. Can one who loves Christ our Lord be content while these heathen mysteries exist, where souls are prostituted to monstrous faceless gods, where God, in place of being called Jesus, is addressed in subhuman terms?

There are higher and less savage cults, but still the Savior's name is unknown to them. To read and inform oneself about our missions is preeminently a true form of charity. What an impetus to prayer that field is. What an enlargement and expansion too!

The danger of a certain narrowness and ingrowing is very real, and — let's be frank! the religious life can become trivial.

The Religious suffers from it now and then: her horizon does not expand, her perspective is too narrow, and things become unbearable — trivial customs and changes, slight relations.

Sometimes she is unaware of it and then, little by little, her soul becomes shrunken and withdrawn. There is a paradox here which is almost incomprehensible in view of the greatness of the religious vocation; for it is an extraordinary situation in a soul claimed by God for himself and enlarged by the inpouring of his love. If she has ceded to her spouse her situation in the world, then all of her ought to belong to him; and what was hers ought to be his in the same proportion to use and exploit as he pleases.

What is tragically wrong is a soul's letting itself shrink to ordinary dimensions. Such a soul must flee its unnatural cage, take to the air, and let herself be carried away by the love which unites her to God, and float on the tides ceaselessly drawn by his love.

Devotion, love, and care for missions is one of the soundest ways by which a Religious can expand her heart and spirit to the size of the grace given her by her proper vocation. In reaching the width, she will discover the depth of *"Christ's love which surpasses knowledge"* (Eph. 3, 17).

By this means, she will be certain of having and giving a heart as big as the world, a heart that belongs to God, and a sure sign that he reigns in her.

Much better and more exactly, thanks to missions, she will be able to discover in the humblest aspects of her life how great God has made her heart grow.

This will be a help to her daily routine and even to the slightest duties.